Discover ...

Topics for Advanced Learners
Series Editor: Klaus Hinz

Distant Neighbours. Projects in Intercultural Learning

Teachers' Book

By Karl Heinz Wagner
with Anja Beuter and Peter Dieckow

Best. Nr. 40071 1

Verlag Ferdinand Schöningh

Sprachliche Betreuung: Susan Ashworth-Fiedler

Website
www.schoeningh.de

E-Mail
info@schoeningh.de

Gedruckt auf umweltfreundlichem, chlorfrei gebleichtem Papier.

This is to thank the students in my class on 'Distant Neighbours' at the University of Köln. Their contributions helped in many ways to make both the Students' Book and the Teachers' Book learner-centered and practice-oriented. Above all, I owe special thanks to Peggy and David Pennock for offering their advice on the concept and the material of the book and for proof-reading the manuscript.

Umschlaggestaltung: Veronika Wypior

(Verlag Ferdinand Schöningh, Jühenplatz 1, 33098 Paderborn)

Printed in Germany.
Gesamtherstellung: Ferdinand Schöningh, Paderborn.

Druck 5 4 3 2 1 Jahr 04 03 02 01 00

ISBN 3-506-40071-1

Alle deutschsprachigen Teile dieses Werks folgen der reformierten Rechtschreibung und Zeichensetzung.

Inhaltsverzeichnis

Discover ... : Zielsetzung und methodischer Ansatz

Die Themenheftreihe *Discover* ... richtet sich an Schülerinnen und Schüler der Sekundarstufe II und bereitet in Anlehnung an den Themenkatalog der Richtlinien Englisch landeskundliche oder allgemeine, Jugendliche interessierende Themen methodisch-didaktisch auf. Die Verfahrensweise lehnt sich an neuere lernpsychologische Erkenntnisse an. Das besondere Merkmal liegt in der Bearbeitung der Texte anhand von *pre-reading*, *while-reading* und *post-reading*-Aufgaben.

Pre-Reading-Aufgaben führen zum Text, Thema oder Problem hin. Forschungsergebnisse belegen, dass eine interessante Texteröffnung einen positiven Einfluss auf die Textbegegnung hat. Die *pre-reading*-Aufgaben konkretisieren zudem besonders das Vorwissen und bauen Erwartungshaltungen auf. Spezifische *pre-reading*-Aufgaben finden sich in Form von Bild/Text-Collagen auf der in ein Kapitel einführenden *„Start here"*-Seite.

Beim ersten fortlaufenden Lesen kommen unterschiedliche textverarbeitende Operationen ins Spiel. Da hierzu in der Regel nur begrenzte Zeit zur Verfügung steht, ist eine Hilfstätigkeit darin zu sehen, beim Lesen von Zeit zu Zeit innezuhalten um auf das bereits Gelesene zurückzublicken. Durch das verlangsamte Lesetempo können intensivere Interaktionen zwischen Leser und Text stattfinden. Reflexions- und Verstehenshilfen finden sich in *Discover* ... in den *while-reading*-Aufgaben und Beobachtungsanleitungen in der Randspalte. Sie begleiten den Lesevorgang und dienen gleichsam als *navigational aid*. Mit ihrer Hilfe wird das Verständnis der Oberflächenstruktur des Textes sichergestellt. Diese methodische Neuheit wird durch ein besonderes Layout, durch die Unterteilung der Seite in eine Textspalte und eine die *while-reading*-Aufgaben enthaltende Randspalte ermöglicht. Die mit Pfeilen versehenen Aufgaben begleiten den Lesevorgang. Sie haben vorwärtsweisenden, rückverweisenden oder statarischen Charakter. Ein nach unten weisender Pfeil (⮟) verknüpft die Aufgabe mit dem nachfolgenden Text als so genannte Beobachtungsanleitung. Eine mit einem nach innen gerichteten Pfeil (⮜) versehene Aufgabe bezieht sich auf die betreffende Textstelle und ein nach oben weisender Pfeil (⮝) zeigt an, dass sich die Aufgabe auf den gerade gelesenen Textteil bezieht und man sich rückblickend Klarheit über das Textverständnis verschaffen soll.

Alternativ zum *guided reading* können die Aufgaben der Randspalte auch erst nach dem Lesen mündlich oder schriftlich beantwortet werden; ihnen kommt dann die Funktion der üblichen *comprehension questions* zur Überprüfung des Textverständnisses zu. In diesem Fall überlesen die Schüler während des ersten Durchgangs die Fragen und Aufgaben zunächst.

Die sich an den Text anschließenden *Activities* sind vertiefender Natur. Sie beziehen sich auf die kreative Textproduktion sowie auf die Interpretation im weitesten Sinn. Damit wird auch der textanalytische Zugriff geschult.

Die Kombination von *pre-reading-*, *while-reading-*, und *after-reading-assignments (activities)* ermöglicht eine an neuesten lernpsychologischen und methodischen Erkenntnissen orientierte Textbearbeitung im Sinne einer vermittelnden Methode, bei der Leser und Text gleichermaßen den ihnen zukommenden Stellenwert erhalten.

Teil I

Discover ... Distant Neighbours: Projects in Intercultural Learning: Die didaktische Konzeption

Die didaktische Konzeption

Das Thema „Distant Neighbours. Projects in Intercultural Learning" im Englischunterricht

Der Begriff *global* ist in aller Munde, und ein Unterricht, der die Zeichen der Zeit erkennt und deuten helfen will, muss ihn auf seine Tragfähigkeit überprüfen und nach den didaktischen Konsequenzen fragen. Englischunterricht im neuen Jahrtausend wird sich daran messen lassen müssen, wie weit er interkulturelles Verstehen, partnerschaftliche Einstellung und Kooperationswilligkeit und -fähigkeit fördert, indem er fundamentale Gemeinsamkeiten in Denken, Fühlen und Handeln aufdeckt, zugleich aber auch gravierende Unterschiede und Andersartigkeit nicht nur bewusst, sondern als Wert erfahrbar macht. Bewusste Erfahrung der Fremdheit nicht im Sinne von besser oder schlechter, sondern eben als verschieden und anders, führt letztlich auch zu einem vertieften Verstehen seiner selbst. So kann dieses Heft auch ein inhaltlicher Bezugspunkt in einem *Global-Issues-Project* im Rahmen der Friedenserziehung sein.

Manche Themen, Inhalte und Schwerpunkte einer eher konventionellen Landeskunde findet der Leser in *Distant Neighbours* wieder, z.B. in der Konzentration auf die USA mit ihren Regionen, ethnischen Gruppen, *mind-forming concepts* wie *American Dream*, *melting pot*, *salad bowl* oder *multi-ethnic society*. Neu aber ist der Ansatz, die Schwierigkeit gelebter Multikulturalität und Multiethnizität für die in den USA lebenden Menschen bewusst und vor allem in ihrer Tragweite für den deutschen Leser begreiflich zu machen.

Die USA als klassisches Einwanderungsland sind der didaktische Idealfall, an dem sich eine Kultur als Konglomerat, als Symbiose der verschiedenen Regionen, Ethnien, Historien und darauf gegründeten kulturellen Identitäten beschreiben lässt, was sich in der Wortschöpfung der *hyphenated Americans* niedergeschlagen hat.

Die Konzentration auf die Einwanderungswellen der *Asian-Americans* und *Mexican-Americans* spiegelt den augenblicklichen Stand, trägt vor allem der Entwicklung in den letzten beiden Jahrzehnten sowohl quantitativ, was die Einwanderungszahlen, als auch qualitativ, was die Nachhaltigkeit in der öffentlichen Wahrnehmung angeht, Rechnung. Die *Jewish-Americans*, hier die vor der Verfolgung durch die Nationalsozialisten ins amerikanische Exil geflohenen Juden aus Deutschland, repräsentieren natürlich einmal die späte Einwanderungswelle der Europäer; ihre Bedeutung aber gerade für deutsche Schülerinnen und Schüler liegt in der Reflexion der Autoren zugleich über ihre amerikanische *und* deutsche Identität und ihre spezifische Rolle als deutsche Juden. Indem ihre Beiträge zur Entwicklung eines kritischen amerikanischen Kulturbewusstseins erkennbar werden, wird über das den Menschen zugefügte Unrecht hinaus auch deutlich, welcher Verlust durch die Vertreibung der Juden dem deutschen Kulturleben zugefügt wurde.

Textauswahl

Die ersten drei Kapitel enthalten Auszüge aus Romanen der letzten Jahre, denen die Thematisierung des interkulturellen Konflikts gemeinsam ist. Sie stellen so etwas wie eine Antwort der Literatur auf die Frage nach dem Umgang miteinander in einer immer rascher zusammenwachsenden Welt dar. Gemeinsam ist ihnen auch ein skeptischer Optimismus, der die Probleme nicht verdeckt, sondern durch ihre schonungslose Offenlegung zu ihrer Bewältigung beizutragen hofft.

Die beiden ersten Kapitel konzentrieren sich auf die beiden wichtigsten Einwanderungsgruppen der Gegenwart, die *Asian-Americans* und die *Mexican-Americans*, während das dritte Kapitel mit Einblicken in jüdische Schicksale die Brücke in die jüngere Vergangenheit und das Deutschland des Dritten Reiches schlägt.

Die literarischen Texte werden durch Kurzbiografien und Fallstudien erweitert und vertieft und sollten im Unterricht durch exemplarische Verfilmungen einschließlich *audio-books* und *songs*, die jeweils zu den Basistexten vorliegen, im Sinne der *media-literacy* ergänzt werden.

Neu ist die Einbeziehung populärwissenschaftlicher Beiträge aus der Reiseliteratur, die sich z.T. auf originelle Weise mit auch heute noch gängigen Vorurteilen und Klischees auseinander setzen. Darauf aufbauend finden sich im letzten Kapitel kulturpsychologische Reflexionen zu Herkunft und Bedeutung gemeinschaftsbedingter Kulturstandards und Auszüge aus Trainingsprogrammen aus dem internationalen Managertraining, die praktische Konsequenzen aus den unterschiedlichen Kulturstandards zu ziehen versuchen. Sie bieten sich als Grundlage für das Selbststudium und als Anregung zu selbst gesteuertem Lernen an, dessen Ergebnisse im abschließenden Vergleich relativiert und dadurch differenziert betrachtet werden können.

Textdidaktisch geht es bei den literarischen Texten einmal um die Berücksichtigung aller drei traditionellen Gattungen durch lyrische, narrative und dramatische Beispiele, hier vertreten durch den Auszug aus einem *film-script*. Unter den Sachexten finden sich Textformvarianten von der wissenschaftlichen Abhandlung über Essay und Satire bis hin zur Transkription eines Interviews. Meist stammen die Beiträge aus dem letzten Jahrzehnt, im Fall der *Jewish-Americans* aber war es notwendig, die historische Perspektive zu berücksichtigen. Zudem ist der Textbegriff sehr extensiv ausgelegt, um auch Hörtexte und Kartenmaterial, Bilder, Fotos, Cartoons und Stiche, sozusagen optische „Texte", mit einzubeziehen. Anders als bei einer kapitelweisen Progression stellen die Kapitel hier unterschiedliche thematische Aspekte des Rahmenthemas bzw. unterschiedliche (wissenschafts-) methodische Ansätze wie z.B. philologisch-textexegetische oder sozialwissenschaftlich-empirische Verfahrensweisen vor.

Alle Kapitel wollen nicht zuletzt die Schülerinnen und Schüler anregen, den in ihnen vorgestellten Phänomenen auf den Grund zu gehen, selbst nach weiteren Beispielen (Romanen, Kurzgeschichten, Gedichten oder Songs) zu suchen und Zusammenfassungen, Kritiken oder Collagen in einer Arbeitsmappe (*portfolio*) zu sammeln, Filme oder Fernsehserien oder Cartoons auf das Bild vom Anderen (z.B. auch des Deutschen) hin zu untersuchen und den Kursmitgliedern in geeigneter und motivierender Form, d.h. der *presentation*, vorzustellen. Die einzelnen Kapitel können auch als Ausgangspunkt für Unterrichtsprojekte einschließlich Facharbeit gewählt werden, die allein oder vorzugsweise im Team bearbeitet werden sollten.

Tabellarische Textübersicht

Autor, Text	Inhaltliche Schwerpunkte	Textsorte	Wortzahl
	Chapter 1: At First Sight – On Second Thought		
David Guterson, *Being Japanese-American in Times of War*	• Mutter-Tochter-Beziehung in der Spannung zwischen amerikanischer Gegenwart und japanischer Vergangenheit • kulturelle Identität: Integration versus Abschottung • *torn between two worlds* in Zeiten des Krieges	literarischer Text Romanauszug narrativ *point of view*	ca. 1220
Ronald Bass, *Snow Falling On Cedars* Adapted for the Screen	• Genre-Unterschiede zwischen Roman und Drehbuch • spezifische Möglichkeiten beider Medien, das Thema der interkulturellen Begegnung zu gestalten	literarischer Text Drehbuchauszug	ca. 150
Amy Tan, *All the Englishes I Grew up With*	• Sprache, kulturelle Identität und Integration in eine fremde Kulturgemeinschaft • Wandel des Sprachgefühls im Prozess der Integration • *Linguistic correctness versus communication*	Sachtext *magazine article* subjektiv argumentativ	ca. 465
T. Coraghessan Boyle, *A Samurai in Georgia*	• Image des Samurai als typisch japanisches Klischee • männliche Perspektive: Emigration als Überlebenskampf • Harmonisierung japan. und amerik. Kulturstandards	literarischer Text Romanauszug narrativ	ca. 650
Lan Cao, *In Shopper's Paradise*	• Kaufverhalten als Ausdruck unterschiedl. Lebensgefühls • *Generation gap*: Festhalten am Alten vs. Aufgeschlossenheit für das Neue	literarischer Text essayistisch deskriptiv	ca. 860
Setsuko K., *No Tea, Thank You*	• *culture shock:* Heimkehr als Erfahrung der Entfremdung • Höflichkeit und Ehrlichkeit als soziale Kulturstandards	Autobiografie	ca. 360
	Chapter 2: Im-Migrants – Needed But Not Wanted		
Francisco Jiménez, *Growing up in a Migrant Setting*	• Lebensbedingungen mexikanischer Wanderarbeiter in der kalifornischen Landwirtschaft • Folgen aus der Sicht eines 12-jährigen Mexikaners, insbes. Hoffnungen und Frustrationen hinsichtlich der Schule • Gegenüberstellung von exemplarisch gesehenem Integrationshemmnis und erfolgreichem Einzelschicksal	literarischer Text *excerpt from a semi-autobiographical short story*	ca. 850
Woody Guthrie, *Plane Wreck at Los Gatos*	• Amerikanischer Umgang mit illegalen mexikanischen Wanderarbeitern • die Ballade als Mittel der Gesellschaftskritik • problematisierende Betrachtung mit interkultureller Perspektive: das personifizierte Amerika als Leitstimme der Kritik	literarischer Text *folk song, ballad*	ca. 250
T.C. Boyle, *They're Mexicans – Bad for Business*	• Arbeit suchende Mexikaner in der kalifornischen Großstadt • Folgen aus der Sicht einer weißen amerikanischen Geschäftsfrau • Gegenüberstellung von aktuellen demographischen Prognosen und historischen Zusammenhängen	literarischer Text *excerpt from a novel*	ca. 920
Robert Frost, *Mending Wall*	• Grundfrage nach dem Sinn und Zweck von Grenzen • das anekdotische Erzählgedicht als Mittel der Auseinandersetzung mit Grundfragen menschlichen Zusammenlebens • widersprüchliche Antworten als Grundhaltungen der *individual observation* und der *social experience*	literarischer Text *poem*	ca. 390

Autor, Text	Inhaltliche Schwerpunkte	Textsorte	Wort-zahl
	Chapter 3: The Limits of Mutual Understanding		
Albert Einstein *The Americans and the Europeans*	• Vergleich des Charakters der Amerikaner und Europäer • Begründung durch Gesellschafts- u. Wirtschaftsstruktur • Formulierung der positiven Eindrücke und Wertungen	Sachtext: expositorisch; subjektiv-argumentativ	ca. 1000
W. H. Auden, *Say This City Has Ten Million Souls*	• Verfolgung, Flucht und Todesnot jüdischer Emigranten • Heimat für alle Kreaturen außer den Juden • Klage über Hilflosigkeit und Herzlosigkeit der Menschen	literarischer Text lyr. Mischform: Ballade, „Blues“	ca. 390
Kurt Vonnegut, Jr., *Adam*	• Bedeutung der Geburt eines Kindes nach der Erfahrung des *holocaust* • Verständnislosigkeit der Umwelt gegenüber *the miracle* • Erinnerungskultur und Identität	literarischer Text *modern Jewish-American short story*	ca. 2700
Alan Isler, *We Were Germans*	• Episode der deutsch-amerikanischen Familiengeschichte • *Jewish-German identity: misunderstanding and guilt* • Variation der Schuldfrage: *Burden of survival*	literarischer Text *an episode: excerpt from a novel*	ca. 1500
Art Spiegelman, *Maus. A Survivor's Tale*	• Aufwachsen als jüdisches Kind in den USA: Erinnerung • Rolle des getöteten Bruders, Leben der Eltern im KZ • Schuldfrage als Ausdruck des Mitleidens • (Un)Vereinbarkeit von *holocaust*, Auschwitz und *comic*	populärer literarischer Bild-Text moralischer und ästhet. Grenzfall	ca. 400
	Chapter 4: Fears and Hopes – Mind-Shaping and Habit-Forming		
Stefan Zeidenitz, Ben Barkow, *The Germans – How They See Others and Themselves*	• Deutsche Sichtweise anderer Nationen (Heterostereotype) • Deutsche sehen sich selbst (Autostereotype) • Reiseführer als intellektuelle Provokation	Sachtext populäre Kulturpsychologie: subjektiv-impressionistisch	ca. 550
Richard Lord, *German Characteristics*	• *The German paradox: high achievers but insecure* • *the effects of Nazi experience on the Germans* • *the nightmare in the interaction with our neighbours*	Sachtext *cultural, historical essay*	ca. 620
George Mikes, *Manners and Mannerisms – The English and the Germans*	• *Episode illustrating English and German behaviour* • *description of English attitudes and conventions* • *critical (satirical) contrast with German behaviour*	*humorous literature: satire exaggerated and critical*	ca. 680
Karl Markowsky, Alexander Thomas, *History and Culture Standards*	• Darlegung der kulturpsychologischen Erkenntnismethode • Entwicklung der Theorie aus dem empirischen Ansatz • Einbeziehung des Kontext- und Weltwissens der Schüler • historische Begründung des Erklärungsversuches	populärwissenschaftlicher Text deskriptiv, argumentativ, handlungsorientiert	ca. 1500
Roger E. Axtell, Tami Briggs, Margaret Corcoran, Beth Lamb, *Testing Your Culture-Gender Awareness*	• Drei Beispiele von *Applied Cultural Psychology* • Quiz zur Frauenrolle in *international business* • *evaluation of your own culture-gender awareness* • *positive or negative feedback and change of attitude*	Fallstudien aus Managementtraining: Auswahlantworten	ca. 800
European and American Cultural Behaviours: How We Perceive Each Other	• Auflistung zentraler amerikanischer Verhaltensmuster • Kontrastierung mit entsprechendem europ.-dt. Verhalten • Beurteilung der Verhaltensweisen durch die jeweils Anderen • Kontrastierung mit der jeweiligen Selbsteinschätzung • Aufforderungscharakter: Überprüfung der eigenen Einstellung und Haltung	Trainingsprogramm Gegenüberstellung von amerik. und europ. Verhaltensweisen vor dem Hintergrund von Kulturstandards	ca. 1000

Integration des Heftes in größere thematische Zusammenhänge

Das Heft ist 1. eine ideale Ergänzung von Lernsequenzen mit amerikakundlicher Schwerpunktsetzung, 2. eine optimale Vorbereitung auf Unterrichtsreihen im Anschluss an die Besprechung der Romane von T. C. Boyle (s. auch das kürzlich erschienene Unterrichtsmodell zu *„The Tortilla Curtain"*, Reihe „EinFach Englisch", Schöningh Verlag, Best.-Nr. 41203-5), Lan Cao, D. Guterson und A. Isler, die hier nur mit Auszügen vorgestellt sind, 3. eine sinnvolle Vor- oder Nachbereitung einer Lernsequenz, die der Rolle ethnischer Gruppen z.B. in Großbritannien im Rahmen der Besprechung von Romanen von H. Kureishi oder der Short-Story-Sammlung *Many Voices – Many Cultures* nachgeht, und bietet schließlich eine grundlegende Zusammenfassung von Fragen nach kultureller Identität, Vorurteilsproblematik und Problematisierung von Fremd- und Eigenwahrnehmung oder *mainstream* und *minorities* als Ausgangs- oder Zielpunkt eines *Global-Issues-Project* an.
Das Heft stellt mit den Romanauszügen repräsentativ vier Regionen der USA vor, den Osten, Nordwesten, Westen und Süden. Es liegt nahe, dem Zusammenhang zwischen Region und literarischen Äußerungen nachzugehen, neue Regionen und ihre Literatur zu entdecken. Ferner bietet es sich an, den Blick auf zwei andere ethnische Gruppen zu lenken und nach der Andersartigkeit ihrer Schicksale und den literarischen Spuren zu fragen: die *Native-Americans* und die *African-Americans*.
Im Rahmen eines *American-Studies-Project* bietet sich das Heft als Begleitmaterial zu einer Unterrichtsreihe an, die Lebensformen oder Einzelschicksalen und ihrer Darstellung in Literatur, Film, Musik und *material culture/life-style* nachgeht und mit Beispielen aus der eigenen Kultur vergleicht. Dabei sollten die eigenen Lebens- oder Leseerfahrungen im Umgang mit Menschen und Institutionen in den USA ebenso Berücksichtigung finden wie die Analyse kritischer Interaktionen in den Beispielen aus den Trainingsprogrammen. Unter dem Gesichtspunkt der Interdisziplinarität ließe sich beispielsweise etwa in Verbindung mit Christoph Meckels *Ein unbekannter Mensch* (1999) das gegenseitige (literarische) Bild vergleichen oder im Zusammenhang mit Bernhard Schlinks *Der Vorleser* (1995, s. Unterrichtsmodell der Reihe „EinFach Deutsch", Best.-Nr. 22281-3) der Frage nachgehen, wieso dieser Roman in der Übersetzung in den USA 1999 zur literarischen Sensation und zum Bestseller wurde.

Anbindung an Ganzschriften

The Hyphenated Americans

- T. Coraghessan Boyle: *East Is East*
- T. Coraghessan Boyle: *The Tortilla Curtain*
- Lan Cao: *Monkey Bridge*
- David Guterson: *Snow Falling on Cedars*
- Alan Isler: *The Prince of West End Avenue*

Im Vergleich mit **Native Americans**:
- Michael Blake: *Dances with Wolves*

Im Vergleich mit **African-Americans**:
- Toni Morrison: *Jazz*

Living in and looking at a different culture

- Julian Barnes: "The Visitors". In: *A History of the World in 10 1/2 Chapters.*
  Geschichte eines britischen Kunsthistorikers, der von der Entführung eines Kreuzfahrtschiffs durch Terroristen berichtet, die auf der Suche nach Juden unter den internationalen Passagieren sind.
- Lan Cao: *Monkey Bridge*
  Biografie einer jungen vietnamesischen Einwanderin in die USA
- John LeCarré: *A Small Town in Germany*
  Blick auf das Bonn der 68er-Jahre aus der Perspektive britischer Diplomaten und Geheimdienstler
- Donna Leon: *Death at La Fenice*
  Commissario Brunetti aus Venedig klärt den Mord an einem deutschen Stardirigenten (mit NS-Vergangenheit) auf.
- Peter Mayle: *Anything Considered*
  Ein britischer Junggeselle wird in einen Kriminalfall der internationalen haute cuisine in der Provence verwickelt, den er mit Hilfe einer jungen Amerikanerin löst.
- Barbara Korte und Claudia Sternberg (ed.): *Many Voices – Many Cultures. Multicultural British Short Stories*
- Hanif Kureishi: *The Buddha of Suburbia*
  Geschichte des jungen Karim Amir, "an Englishman born and bred, almost", und seiner Familie, speziell seines Vaters, in der multikulturellen Atmosphäre Londons
- Magdalen Nabb: Death of a Dutchman
  Der Tod eines holländischen, mit einer Engländerin verheirateten Juweliers in Florenz wird von einem sizilianischen Wachtmeister aufgeklärt, der selbst Fremder in der Touristenmetropole ist.

Fächerübergreifend, als Grundlage für eine Facharbeit:

- Christoph Meckel: *Ein unbekannter Mensch*
  Poetisches Porträt seines Freundes, eines Bauern aus der Haute Provence
- Bernhard Schlink: *Der Vorleser*
  Ein Junge gerät in den Bann einer älteren Frau, die er später als Angeklagte in einem NS-Mordprozess wieder trifft. Nach ihrer Verurteilung schickt er ihr, da sie sich zu lesen weigert, von sich selbst besprochene Kassetten mit literarischen Werken ins Gefängnis.

Weiterführende Literatur

- Klaus Ahleim, Bardo Heger: *Vorurteile und Fremdenfeindlichkeit.* Wochenschau Verlag, Schwalbach/Ts., 1998
- Wesley Brown, Amy Ling: *Imagining America.* Stories from the Promised Land. Persea Books, New York, 1991
- Joel Garreau: *The Nine Nations of America.* Avon Books, New York, 1981

- Joann Faung Jean Lee: *Asian Americans.* The New Press, New York, 1997
- Ana Lopez: *Growing up Chicana/o*. Avon Books, New York, 1993
- Andrea Müller, Alexander Thomas: *Interkulturelles Orientierungstraining für die USA.* Breitenbach Verlag, Saarbrücken/Fort Lauderdale, Fla., 1991
- Peter Novick: *The Holocaust in American Life.* Houghton Mifflin Company, Boston/New York, 1999
- Ansgar und Vera Nünning: *Der Deutsche an sich.* Deutscher Taschenbuch Verlag, München, 1994
- Neal R. Peirce, Jerry Hagstrom: *The Book of America. Inside Fifty States Today.* W. W. Norton, New York, 1983
- Robert K. Shirer: *Kulturelle Begegnungen – Cross Cultural Mini-Dramas.* National Textbook Company, Lincolnwood, Ill., 1994 (1981)
- Thomas Sowell: *Race and Culture. A World View.* Basic Books Harper Collins, New York, 1994
- Thomas Sowell: *Migration and Cultures.* Basic Books Harper Collins, New York, 1996
- Paul Watzlawick: *Gebrauchsanweisung für Amerika.* Piper, München, ^{19}1996

Teil II

Discover… Distant Neighbours. Projects in Intercultural Learning: Das Schülerbuch im Unterricht

Getting started

In einem ***brainstorming*** Sammeln erster Bildeindrücke von den zwölf Hühnchen; Gruppierung dieser Eindrücke und Assoziationen unter den Aspekten *identification and classification* mit folgenden möglichen und sinnvollen Zuordnungen: ***nationalities*** *such as English, US-American, Dutch, Japanese/Chinese, French, Swiss, Italian*; ***gender*** *such as Arab woman, Japanese/Chinese woman;* ***regions*** *such as Bavaria, for non-Germans: German;* **continents** *such as: Africa, Asia, America*; **religions** *such as: Muslim/Islamic;* ferner: *classification according to* ***physical appearance, dress, eating habits, accessories, etc.***
Lehrgespräch über *nature and effect of prejudices, clichés, stereotypes: supplying orientation in an unknown world but also (if unreflected) barring us from getting to know people, etc. really …*; hier noch keine Differenzierung etwa zwischen Vorurteil, Klischee und (Auto-/Hetero-)Stereotyp; spätere Erarbeitung an den vorgelegten Texten und Aufgaben.
Entweder kurze **Stillarbeit** oder **Partnerarbeit**: *Jot down/explain to your partner how you understand the biblical quotation.*
Hausaufgabe: *Explain the function of the chicken at the bottom left;* oder: *Find more examples of prejudices, clichés, stereotypes in and around you (bring in pictures, cartoons, posters, collect jokes, etc.).*

Chapter 1: At First Sight – On Second Thought

Vorbemerkungen zum Kapitel

Im Zentrum dieses Kapitels steht die vielfach belastete Beziehung zwischen amerikanischer und japanischer Kultur. Eine Auswahl literarischer und expositorischer Texte stellt Lebensauffassungen der *Asian-Americans* vor. Sie liegen zwischen vollständiger Aneignung amerikanischer Werte und Normen und Verinnerlichung des *American way of life* bei gleichzeitiger Aufgabe der eigenen kulturellen Identität einerseits und dem Versuch andererseits, innerhalb einer als minderwertig und feindlich empfundenen Fremdkultur die eigene Herkunft und deren Kulturstandards zu bewahren.

Start here

In the back of our minds p. 5

Look at the three pictures below. What do they illustrate?

Die Karikatur fordert dazu auf, sich mit der unterschiedlichen Wahrnehmung (Eigen- und Fremdwahrnehmung) von Nationen und Kulturen auseinander zu setzen.
Der Cartoon *Getting Along With the Chinese for Fun and Profit* verdeutlicht den Einfluss von Images von Völkern und Nationen auf die Art, wie wir Kulturen, die sich von der unseren unterscheiden, begegnen: Ein offensichtlich zielstrebiger, dynamischer amerikanischer Geschäftsmann und ein vermeintlich reservierter, zurückhaltender Chinese treffen einander zum ersten Mal. Ihre ganz unterschiedlichen Verhaltensweisen verstärken im jeweiligen Gesprächspartner die geläufigen Stereotypen vom Amerikaner bzw. Chinesen, was in den „Gedankenblasen" des zweiten Bildes noch unterstrichen wird. Während der chinesische Geschäftsmann sich in seinem Vorurteil vom Amerikaner als einem unzivilisierten Wilden bestätigt fühlt, reduzieren die Assoziationen des Amerikaners ganz China auf das Klischee vom weisen, entrückten Mandarin.

Being Japanese-American in Times of War David Guterson

Author

David Guterson, born in Seattle in 1956, began as a journalist writing for different magazines. In 1995 his widely acclaimed debut novel *Snow Falling on Cedars* won him the PEN/Faulkner Award.

Synopsis of the text

The female protagonist Hatsue and her mother Fujiko reflect on the situation of the Japanese living in a foreign country. While Fujiko, whose perspective is focused on in the dominantly narrative first half of the text, represents the idea of a total separation of cultures, Hatsue's position is that of being completely integrated into the country she was born in and she identifies with. These incompatible views are part of a typical mother-daughter conflict, in which the daughter's position is influenced by her feelings of love and respect for her mother.

Unterrichts-empfehlungen

Vorbemerkungen
Der Textauszug ermöglicht verschiedene Schwerpunktsetzungen. Auf der Ebene der Figurenkonstellation bietet sich eine Analyse des komplizierten Mutter-Tochter-Verhältnisses an (vgl. Dialogstruktur). Auf der Ebene der Gestaltung interkulturell relevanter Themen steht Integration versus Segregation und folglich Isolation im Mittelpunkt. Schließlich liegt auch die Einbeziehung der historischen Perspektive nahe, die das diffizile Verhältnis zwischen US-Amerikanern und japanischen Einwanderern als eine Folge des Zweiten Weltkrieges und insbesondere des japanischen Angriffs auf Pearl Harbour zu erklären sucht. Die ausschließlich weibliche Perspektive stellt einen Vorteil insofern dar, als sich hierdurch interpretatorische Leerstellen ergeben, die von den Schülerinnen und Schülern in handlungsorientierter Aktivität gefüllt werden können.

1. Schwerpunkt
Nach der Analyse der gegensätzlichen Figurenperspektiven kann die Relevanz der angebotenen Lebensmodelle für Interkulturalität untersucht werden: Inwieweit stellt die von Fujiko propagierte Aufrechterhaltung der Eigenkultur ein praktikables Modell zum Überleben in einer fremden Kulturgemeinschaft dar? Impliziert Hatsues Wille zur völligen Integration tatsächlich eine Verleugnung der eigenen Identität, wie Fujiko befürchtet?

2. Schwerpunkt
Ein zweiter Schwerpunkt kann auf Hatsues Perspektive liegen, die sich im Verlauf des Dialoges ändert und durch das Stilmittel z.B. der *erlebten Rede* in ihrer Wandlung deutlich gemacht wird.

3. Schwerpunkt
Ein dritter Schwerpunkt kann die Frage nach der Gestaltung des geschichtlichen Hintergrunds sein, der die Vereinsamung und innere Isolation Fujikos und ihre negative Einschätzung der Amerikaner verständlich macht: *What do we learn about the relationship between Americans and Asians as it was during World War II through Guterson's fictional presentation?*

Assignments

Pre-reading task

Think of some difficulties that might arise when Japanese and American people live together.

Before you read p. 6

While the Americans strongly believe in the idea that every person has a right to pursue his/her own happiness, which leads to the conviction that anything is possible if you only try hard enough (*from rags to riches, from dishwasher to millionaire)*, people in Japan see human beings as part of a greater community. While Americans view values such as ambition, competitiveness and self-confidence as positive, in Japan they are condemned as counteracting the idea of community.

While-reading tasks

p. 6 ➤ *Odyssey:* Check the term and point out what it tells you.

The term is derived from Homer's epic *Odyssey*, the story of Ulysses' return from the war against Troy. Here, the term *odyssey* indicates that emigration is always a difficult and threatening venture the consequences of which remain unknown. Those who want to start a new life successfully have to be strong and capable of enduring hard times and at the same time keep up hope and optimism.

p. 6 ➤ Why does Fujiko use this term *(hakujin)*?

Fujiko's usage of the Japanese word for Americans shows that she does not regard herself as a part of the country she lives in and indicates her contempt for the American culture as being inferior.

p. 7 ➤ "Darkness in the hearts of the *hakujin*." What does Fujiko want to express?

The expression refers to Fujiko's elaboration on the Japanese search for a union with the Greater Life and the Americans' lack of such a religious basis for their existence.

p. 7 ➤ Where does Fujiko see the greatest differences between the Japanese and the American culture? Name some of the cultural values involved.

Modesty ("We know our egos are nothing. […] We bend our heads, we bow and are silent.") vs. egoism; individualism vs. sense of community; separateness and aloneness vs. union and collectiveness.

p. 8 ➤ Why does Hatsue suddenly feel ashamed of herself?

At one point of the conversation Hatsue realizes the universal truth in what her mother says. In neglecting her Japanese origin, she also neglects everything her parents fought for and intended to pass on to her: purity, being religious, modesty, etc. In Freudian terms, Hatsue's superego suddenly gets hold of her and makes her regret everything she claimed before.

Activities

Images and associations p. 8 ➤

1. Look at the photograph on the following page. What associations does it evoke?

Living in two worlds, alienation from your roots, trying to adapt to a new world, being lost, being terrified, feeling of utter loneliness, etc.

2. Remember Fujiko described her journey from Japan to America as an *odyssey*. Comment on this image taking the photograph into account.

Like Ulysses' odyssey, a long, dangerous journey into a far away world, strange and hostile with little hope of finding one's home, etc.

Characters and interaction of characters p. 9

1. Comment on the personalities of Fujiko and Hatsue. In what way do they differ from one another, in what way do they resemble each other?

Fujiko proposes they should keep up their own cultural identity, even if this means isolation in a foreign country. Hatsue tends to assimilate the American culture, a culture she identifies with since she was born in America. The reason for Fujiko's position is her belief that the Americans lack a sense of community, essential for the Japanese.

2. Characterize the relationship between mother and daughter. Do they interact as partners with equal rights?

No. Fujiko is in a much more powerful position and claims the right to tell her daughter how to live her life. This makes her daughter reconsider her opinion. Though Fujiko acknowledges the fact that her daughter is a grown-up person, she nevertheless uses her traditional role as a mother to convince Hatsue that what she thinks is wrong and leads to self-alienation.

3. Outline Fujiko's position: what is her idea of living among the Americans? Compare it with Hatsue's opinion.

Fujiko wants to reduce interaction with the Americans to those encounters absolutely necessary. It is her ideal to maintain her Japanese origin and, accordingly, Japanese norms, values and standards; isolation and loneliness are most willingly accepted. Hatsue regards herself as an American since she was born and raised in America and sees no sense in sticking to her Japanese roots.

Personal opinion p. 9

Which position do you share, which do you reject? Give reasons for your argument and discuss it in class.

The students should make a list of arguments for their position and then compare their findings in small groups. A speaker should be appointed by each group to present the results to open a discussion.

Focusing on perspective p. 9

The story is narrated by the so-called omniscient narrator. Nevertheless, the reader seems to be drawn to Hatsue's perspective rather than to Fujiko's. Can you explain why?

The reader sees everything through Hatsue's eyes. She is the protagonist of the novel and at the same time the focalizer of what happens and of what is said between mother and daughter.

Interpretation of character through subjective writing p. 9

1. *From a female perspective*. Obviously Hatsue seems to be *torn between two worlds*. Imagine she would sit down at her desk that same evening and write into her diary about the things that were said, her hopes and fears, her disappointments and plans and her secret thoughts. Write what she might have written.

A diary entry from Hatsue's point of view will be highly subjective and intimate and might concentrate on her mixed feelings, first on her self-confident claim to be a part of the US, later her feelings of regret and shame. Accordingly, one can focus on possible plans and sketch an optimistic outlook for the woman, or one might stress Hatsue's disappointments and her guilty conscience and so come up with a more pessimistic view.

2. *From a male perspective*. Imagine you have been secretly listening to Hatsue's and Fujiko's conversation as Hatsue's friend. Jot down your spontaneous reaction: what would you advise Hatsue to do? Comment on the two women's conflict from a male position. Write a letter to Hatsue.

Since the text presents a conflict between mother and daughter and so an exclusively female perspective, it might be interesting to judge the situation from a male point of view. In a way, being involved as Hatsue's friend but not being a part of the conflict, a male outsider might come up with completely new ideas and more objective and reasonable strategies as to how the problem could be solved. One can support Hatsue in her own opinion and come up with new arguments to strengthen her position or choose to explain Fujiko's position and try to convince Hatsue that her mother is right in her own way and that she must try to find a compromise – or leave.

Snow Falling on Cedars Adapted for the Screen

Ronald Bass

Author

Ronald Bass wrote the script for the film based on Guterson's novel. It was released in 2000.

Synopsis of the text

The excerpt taken from Ronald Bass' screenplay focuses on that part of the conversation between Hatsue and Fujiko that deals with the central difference between the Americans and the Japanese: *darkness in the hearts of the hakujin* versus *search for union with the Greater Life*.

Unterrichtsempfehlungen

Vorbemerkungen

Auf der Basis der Lektüre des Romansauszugs vermittelt die Behandlung dieser Passage aus dem Drehbuch vor allem genrespezifische Einsichten. Der unterrichtliche Schwerpunkt sollte dem entsprechend auf die Erarbeitung der Unterschiede zwischen narrativem und dramatischem Darstellungsmodus gelegt werden.

Assignments

Pre-reading task

What are the typical characteristics of a screenplay?

dramatic form: dialogue, stage directions.

From novel to screenplay p. 10

Activities

Point out the main formal differences between the passage taken from Guterson's novel and the text above.

Discussing genre p. 10

Narrative form versus dramatic form: inside views of the characters are presented via free indirect style (*erlebte Rede*) in the novel, while they are summarized and so abridged in the stage directions of the screenplay; speeches are reduced to their central messages. The consequence is a more superficial presentation of characters, their mental situation and psychological development in the screenplay.

1. Which aspects did the scriptwriter focus on?

Looking at the content p. 10

The focus lies on Fujiko's estimation of Japanese values in contrast to American ones and Hatsue's attempt to bring in counter-arguments.

2. Does the fact that Hatsue is torn between two worlds become clear? Give reasons for your argument.

No. Hatsue's thought-process from being convinced about her position to doubting it on the basis of her mother's arguments, as it is presented in the novel, isn't made evident at all. She appears to be strong in her identification with the Americans ("I am not part of them. I'm part of here.") and in her opposition to her mother's view.

3. Compare the relationship between the two women as it is presented here with what you found out about them on the basis of the original text. Explain the differences.

Whereas in the novel Hatsue holds the weaker position as being the daughter of a self-confident and strong mother, who makes use of her traditional right to give her daughter advice on how to live her life, the screenplay shows two equally convinced women discussing their opposing positions.

Look at the film scene above. Can you do better? Imagine you were a scriptwriter and you had to transform Guterson's novel into a screenplay, either for theatre or film. Look at the narrative passage on p. 7 again and decide what is necessary to put into the dialogue. Write out this dialogue as well as the stage directions you find appropriate.

Creating your own script p. 10

The students might want to enrich the script with a presentation of Hatsue's thought-process. The task to transform a character's thoughts as narrated in a novel into speeches appropriate for a screenplay and to choose stage directions that support the intended effect gives the students another opportunity to work closely and intensively on that character's perspective.

All the Englishes I Grew up With

Amy Tan

Author

Amy Tan, American writer of Chinese origin, was born in California in 1952, where she grew up surrounded by influences from both Chinese and American culture. Before her best-selling novel *The Joy Luck Club* (for which she won the L. A. Book Award and The National Book Award) was published in 1989, she had different jobs, varying from bartender to counsellor for developmentally disabled children. She now lives and works in San Francisco. Her writings include novels and essays as well as various other short prose and journalistic texts.

Synopsis of the text

Amy Tan reflects on the importance of one's mother tongue and its relevance for one's cultural and national identity. The exploration of her thoughts and feelings while giving a speech in her mother's presence serves as an example to illustrate the false assumption that grammatical correctness is all there is to language. Tan's description of her mother's survival in America without having a perfect command of the English language leads to her insight that there is no such thing as *broken* English and that, in contrast, it is exactly the variety of different usages of language, different accents and different definitions of what is correct that makes language interesting and lively.

Unterrichtsempfehlungen

Vorbemerkungen

Der Text greift die Bedeutung von Sprache für die eigene kulturelle Identität auf und rückt somit einen essentiellen Aspekt von Interkulturalität in den Mittelpunkt des Interesses. Hierdurch werden Schülerinnen und Schüler auf einer sehr persönlichen Ebene angesprochen: sowohl als Muttersprachler als auch vor allem als Lerner einer Fremdsprache.

Assignments

While-reading tasks

p. 11 ➤ Why did the presence of her mother give Amy the feeling that what she was saying sounded wrong?

It was the first time that her mother, who stood out from the intellectual audience Amy normally speaks to, listened to a speech of hers. This evoked new associations in Amy's mind and made her realize the artificiality of her language usage in comparison to her mother's English usage.

p. 12 ➤ Why does Amy find her mother's language "perfectly clear", "perfectly natural"?

She grew up listening to her mother's very personal way of speaking, a mixture of Chinese and English, and so has become used to it over the years. Although native speakers would regard it as "broken" English, she is convinced that her mother has a deeper understanding of things than anybody else.

What does Amy have against the word "broken"? Can you think of any other term?

p. 12

The term "broken" has a purely negative connotation: it is used in order to mark language usage wrong that doesn't follow the grammatical rules. The students might, for example, come up with alternatives such as "personal", "subjective", "individual", or "extraordinary".

Activities

How much does the (correct) use of language signal the integration of a person coming from another country? Discuss in class.

Language and integration
p. 12

Most people consider it a fact that the better one's command of a foreign language, the better he or she will be integrated into that foreign culture since language is an essential part of culture. The text, however, has given evidence of the possibility of having a poor command of English and at the same time being fully integrated into the American culture. The students might want to discuss this question with special reference to the idea that there is no such thing as right or wrong but that it is all a matter of social evaluation and traditional assessment.

Remember Giovanni Trappatoni's speech at a press conference in 1997 in which he criticized German football players (*"Ich habe fertig"*). Try to explain why most Germans reacted in such an extreme way to Trappatoni's mistake. How do *you* react to grammatical incorrectness?

An example
p. 12

Trappatoni's speech combined a highly serious content with a very poor command of the German language. Unfortunately for the speaker, this led to an unintended comic effect that covered up the original message he wanted to convey – namely that the football players in the national league are lazy, egoistic and greedy. The comic effect was reinforced by the fact that Trappatoni's speech was accompanied by strong facial expression and an extreme use of gestures, taken to be typical of Italian speakers.

Language teaching has changed over the past years. Find reasons why the communicative approach is predominant nowadays.

Linguistic correctness vs. communication
p. 12

The nineties are seen as an era of globalisation and communication. Consequently, having a good command of foreign languages has become more and more important. The growing interrelation and interdependence of countries and cultures has led to a mingling of linguistic influences, the origin of which is sometimes difficult to trace. However, society and eventually also education authorities have realized that the ability to communicate successfully with other people, even at the expense of grammatical correctness, cannot be overestimated.

Personal opinion ➤ p. 12

Don't forget: you are learning a second language, too! What is your attitude?

It is to be expected that the students' point of view will vary between the two extremes: communication and correctness.

Writing a comment ➤ p. 12

Write an editorial for a newspaper discussing this issue. Give your article the following title: "Good or bad English – does correctness count?"

When writing an editorial, students learn on at least two different levels: on the one hand, to some extent they aquire media literacy, and, on the other hand, they are encouraged to deal with this question again intensively, having to find and arrange the appropriate arguments to support their position.

A Samurai in Georgia

T. Coraghessan Boyle

Author

T. Coraghessan Boyle is a best-selling novelist and worked as a high school teacher before he began his literary career. Since 1977 he has been a professor of English at the University of Southern California. One of his books, *The Road to Welville*, was made into a big Hollywood movie and made him famous among non-readers as well. He was born in the state of New York and currently lives in Santa Barbara, California.

Synopsis of the text

The text follows a young Japanese seaman swimming towards the shore of the United States. Narrated by the so-called omniscient narrator, the passage nevertheless provides the reader with a large number of inside views of the main character, which are mainly written in free indirect style. Consequently, going over from one cultural community to another – crossing the cultural border, so to speak – is seen from the highly subjective point of view of that character.

Unterrichtsempfehlungen

Vorbemerkungen

Der Textauszug eröffnet den Schülerinnen und Schülern einen Einblick in die männliche Perspektive und rückt das Image des Japaners als Samurai in den Mittelpunkt. Der Schwerpunkt der Textarbeit könnte somit unter Rückgriff auf die zuvor behandelten Textbeispiele auf einen Vergleich zwischen weiblichem und männlichem Umgang mit fremden Kulturen und interkultureller Begegnung gelegt werden. Des Weiteren kann das Zustandekommen des Samurai-Mythos' sowie seine literarische Verarbeitung durch Boyle kritisch in den Blick genommen und durch Hinzuziehung von außerliterarischen, insbesondere geschichtlichen Informationen näher erforscht werden.

Assignments

While-reading tasks

What associations do you come up with when thinking of Samurais? Draw a mindmap.

p. 13

The samurai, originally the escort of the Emperor and his family as well as the nobility, later became direct vassals of shoguns and local princes and, in the 17th century, formed the highest class in Japanese society: its members were mainly recruited from the armed forces, the civil servants and the clergy. The samurai have always had very strict ideas of loyalty, dignity, respect, duty, strength, courage and public reputation – characteristics which are defined in a special code of honour. The students are likely to come up with characteristics such as these since the image of the samurai is widely used in modern movies, especially so-called "Easterns".

Describe Tanaka's state of mind.

p. 13

Tanaka is mentally as well as physically exhausted: his thoughts seem to circle around the wish to be in a warm bed, the desire to eat and the strong need to rest. Eventually, his tiredness and exhaustion appear to result in a strong weariness of life, and he is on the verge of giving up. What keeps him going, though, is his friend Jocho's wise saying that important considerations should be taken lightly, while small matters should be taken seriously. This principle supports Tanaka in his effort to overcome his physical exhaustion and gives him new strength.

What ideas does Tanaka have about the Americans?

p. 14

At first sight, his image corresponds to the typical cliché of the Americans as consumers of fast food and people without any cultural background, ultimately doomed to decay. However, in showing Tanaka entering upon such a highly dangerous trip to America, this country is indirectly depicted as the "promised land", a country which is worth risking one's life for. And, certainly, this is the way Tanaka sees America, even if it is only on a subconscious level.

From where does Tanaka get his power to carry on?

p. 14

Tanaka's mental strength is the result of his Japanese education, especially his having internalised the idea of taking small matters seriously while seeing important questions with a relaxed state of mind – this principle can be seen as being diametrically contrary to the way Westerners handle their lives. However, with this principle in mind, Tanaka is able to suppress his existential doubts and to carry on with a newly acquired lightness and ease.

Activities

Imagine you are a psychologist who has to write a report about Tanaka. What kind of person is he? Is he fit to survive in the United States? Comment on his strengths and weaknesses.

Characterization
p. 14

This task encourages the students to focus on Tanaka's literary characterization and leads to a detailed knowledge of his attitude. Tanaka may be seen as a very strong and self-confident character who is able to overcome physical weaknesses purely by mental strength. This renders him a person who is able to adjust to unknown or even dangerous situations and this, in turn, proves his fitness to survive in a foreign cultural community. On the other hand, the fact that his idea of the Americans seems to be based on typical clichés and stereotypes shows that in spite of his mind's strength and his apparent intellectualism he, nevertheless, is not free from prejudices and false assumptions.

Speculating and predicting p. 14 ➤

Outline Tanaka's first encounter with the Americans: how does he experience his arrival at the American shore? Take notes on what you consider important and write a small text. You may choose the texttype you prefer, e.g. a dialogue between Tanaka and an American or Tanaka's train of thought.

The production of a text presenting Tanaka's first encounter with the Americans may be based on the results of the psychological report. The students have all sorts of possibilities to speculate on the future action: Tanaka might be fascinated or repelled by the attitude and the way of living of the foreign people as well as by his new surroundings. He might realize that his image of the Americans was a mere prejudice that has to be reconsidered and defined anew, but he might just as well find his prejudices to be in accordance with reality. The way the students create Tanaka's arrival in America will depend on their own personal experiences with foreign nationalities and so lead to a subjective interpretation of the text.

In Shopper's Paradise

Lan Cao

Author

Lan Cao left Vietnam in 1975. She lives in New York now where she is a professor of international law at Brooklyn Law School.

Synopsis of the text

In this passage taken from Lan Cao's autobiography *Monkey Bridge* the writer compares the American way of life with that of the Vietnamese, especially the way people manage their everyday life. Staying with her aunt and uncle, young Lan Cao witnesses her aunt's admirable skill and cleverness in doing the shopping. This experience evokes memories of the way people, and especially her mother, go shopping in Vietnam and ultimately leads to general thoughts about the positive and negative aspects of both traditions.

Unterrichtsempfehlungen

Vorbemerkungen
Der Textauszug stellt eine äußerst lebensnahe und sinnliche, d. h. alle Sinne des Lesers ansprechende Beschreibung der vietnamesischen im Gegensatz zur amerikanischen Lebensart dar. Neben einer dominant inhaltlichen Bearbeitung des Textes mit dem Fokus auf dem Vergleich der dargestellten Konventionen bietet sich der Text aufgrund seiner sprachlichen Gestaltung überdies auch für eine intensivierte Vokabelarbeit an.

1. Schwerpunkt
Entsprechend dem Ziel der Erlangung eines möglichst fundierten Textverständnisses sollten die Schülerinnen und Schüler zunächst die dargestellten Gegensätze zwischen „shopping the American way" und den vietnamesischen Einkaufskonventionen herausarbeiten. Hierzu könnte es von Vorteil sein, die von der Autorin zur Charakterisierung der unterschiedlichen Lebensformen verwendeten Adjektive tabellarisch aufzulisten und abschließend auf ihre jeweilige Konnotationen hin zu untersuchen.

2. Schwerpunkt
Basierend auf einer Betrachtung der unterschiedlich konnotierten Lebensweisen sollten die Schülerinnen und Schüler dazu aufgefordert werden, Lan Caos Bewertung der amerikanischen und vietnamesischen Lebensweise zu analysieren. Aufgrund der Tatsache, dass sich die Autorin einer einseitigen Zuweisung von positiven versus negativen Eigenschaften enthält und vereinfachende Stereotypisierungen vermeidet, fordert diese Aufgabe vom Rezipienten eine intensive Auseinandersetzung mit dem Text.

3. Schwerpunkt
Um die anhand des Guterson-Textes exemplarisch gewonnenen Erkenntnisse über die Beschaffenheit einer Mutter-Tochter-Beziehung zweier aus dem asiatischen Kulturraum stammenden Frauen zu erweitern, könnte die in Lan Caos Autobiografie deutlich werdende Beziehung der Autorin zu ihrer Mutter untersucht werden. Dabei dürften den Schülerinnen und Schülern sowohl Gemeinsamkeiten – die Bewunderung für und der Respekt Lan Caos vor ihrer Mutter –, vor allem aber auch Unterschiede auffallen: So ist es hier die Tochter, die im Vergleich zu ihrer Mutter über einen deutlichen Wissens- und Erfahrungsvorsprung verfügt und dabei gleichzeitig eine Position innehat, die es ihr zu erlauben scheint, ihre Mutter von diesem Wissen profitieren zu lassen – ganz offensichtlich ohne traditionelle Machtstrukturen innerhalb der Familie zu verletzen.

4. Schwerpunkt
Wie bereits in den Vorbemerkungen angesprochen, bietet sich der Text aufgrund seiner sinnlichen Wortgewalt und überaus ausschweifenden Metaphorik für eine intensive Wortschatzarbeit an. Die Schülerinnen und Schüler sollten aufgefordert werden zu erklären, inwiefern die spezifische sprachliche Gestaltung des Textes dazu dient, alle Sinne des Rezipienten anzusprechen.

Assignments

Pre-reading tasks

Every picture tells a story ... p. 15

Look at the two photographs below. The one on the left shows an American supermarket, the other one an outdoor market in Asia. Describe the two pictures and state the differences between them.

Exact labelling of food vs. no categorization whatsoever; hygienic packaging and neat arrangement of consumer goods vs. groceries that are left in their natural condition; anonymous atmosphere vs. place where socializing is not only possible but necessary.

Implications p. 15

What do the photos tell you about the American and the Asian way of living? Can you name the different cultural values?

The orderliness of the American supermarket suggests a strong need to make shopping an easy activity that goes off as smoothly and quickly as possible. The outdoor market, on the other hand, indicates that shopping in Vietnam is a social event that fulfils more needs than merely buying and selling: it also offers an opportunity to get into contact with other people. Since there are no fixed prices for the goods, a Vietnamese outdoor market calls for unlimited activity of the customers as well as the sellers. Cultural values: artificiality vs. naturalness; perfectionism vs. easy-going; preservation of anonymity vs. socializing; exact order and cleanliness vs. hearty chaos.

Personal opinion p. 15

Which photo corresponds to your idea of a "shopper's paradise"? Give reasons.

It might be expected that most students will tend to prefer shopping the American way since this is more similar to what they are used to in Germany. But at the same time, some students may well be fascinated by the exoticism and apparent simplicity of the Vietnamese shopping conventions.

While-reading tasks

p. 16

What does "shopping the American way" mean to you?

When thinking of America, huge shopping malls come to mind that seem to offer virtually everything the modern customer wants. While a number of people certainly enjoy this vastness of supply, others might be frightened by its enormity.

p. 16

What does the narrator's mother have against American supermarkets?

She apparently misses the noise and the different smells that make Vietnamese "sky markets" a voluptuous and fascinating place for the senses.

What are typical characteristics of a Vietnamese market? Compare with the atmosphere of an American supermarket as described in the text.

p. 17

see above

Activities

Characterize the relationship between mother and daughter and compare it to the mother-daughter-relationship in *Being Japanese-American in Times of War* as well as in *All the Englishes I Grew up With*.

Variation of mother-daughter-relationship
p. 17

All the relationships are based on a great amount of mutual love and respect. While David Guterson presents mother and daughter as being closely attached to traditional role models, which makes it difficult for the daughter to find her own way, Amy Tan as well as Lan Cao are strong-minded and independent women who are endowed with more experiences than their respective mothers.

Obviously the narrator's mother has more difficulties adjusting to the American way of life than her daughter. Can you explain why?

Generation gap
p. 17

Although it is a truism that young people can adjust to foreign situations more easily than the generation of their parents, it might still be an important aspect worth discussing in class: do the students agree with that point of view or do they know any counter-examples that prove this truism to be a mere cliché?

How does the narrator illustrate the differences between the American and the Vietnamese way of shopping? Explain how the description seems to involve all of the reader's senses.

Focusing on the use of language
p. 17

Lan Cao's language is full of verbs and adjectives that belong to the wordfield "sense" and "feeling": the smell of the goods as well as their appearance is described in great detail, and the way they feel as well as the associations that they are likely to evoke in the customer's mind are presented extensively.

No Tea, Thank You Setsuko K.

Author

Setsuko K., a forty-year-old woman of Japanese origin and mother of two children, has lived in the United States since she and her husband had to move there on account of his job. When the *Asian-American Research Project* did a survey Setsuko K. was among the immigrants being interviewed about the relationship between Americans and Asians in general, and the process of her naturalization, especially. She and her family currently live in a New Jersey suburb.

Synopsis of the text

Setsuko K. reflects on the cultural differences between the United States, the country she lives in, and her home country, Japan. She characterizes the effect of these differing conventions on everyday life and while she claims that she hasn't changed much during the course of the years in America, she still cannot but realize that the long separation from Japan has estranged her from her home.

Unterrichtsempfehlungen

Vorbemerkungen

Indem dieser Text im Unterschied zu den vorangegangenen Textbeispielen die Wiederbegegnung einer Emigrantin mit ihrem Heimatland und die damit verbundenen Eindrücke und Gefühle thematisiert, wird der Kreis dieses ersten Kapitels geschlossen. Die von der in Amerika lebenden Japanerin konstatierte Entfremdung von ihrer ursprünglichen Heimat zeigt die psychologischen Konsequenzen der Emigration auf und bietet Diskussionsstoff insofern, als sich nun die generelle Frage danach stellt, was „Heimat" überhaupt ist und inwieweit kulturelle Identität von nationaler Herkunft bestimmt wird.

Entsprechend der Tatsache, dass dieses Textbeispiel das erste Kapitel abrundet, beziehen sich die anschließenden *Activities* nicht ausschließlich auf diesen Text, sondern ausdrücklich auch auf die vorangegangenen Beispiele interkultureller Begegnung.

1. Schwerpunkt

In einem ersten Analyseschritt sollten die gegensätzlichen kulturellen Standards herausgearbeitet werden: hier die relative Freiheit in der Gestaltung des sozialen Miteinanders, dort die von Setsuko K. als einschränkend empfundene Verpflichtung zum *Socializing*; hier die Auffassung, dass das, was gesagt wird, auch so gemeint ist, dort die aus Gründen der Höflichkeit entstandene Konvention, Angebote zunächst dankend abzulehnen.

2. Schwerpunkt

Daran anschließen sollte sich eine genauere Betrachtung des Umgangs Setsuko K.s mit ihrem neuen sozialen Umfeld in Amerika: eine individuelle Mischung aus selbst gewählter Isolation und Anpassung an die amerikanischen Gepflogenheiten.

3. Schwerpunkt

Abrunden sollte die Textarbeit eine offene Diskussion über die Begriffe „Heimat", „Kulturzugehörigkeit" und „nationale Identität" sowie die Frage, welche gesellschaftlichen und individualpsychologischen Faktoren möglicherweise für deren Beschaffenheit verantwortlich sind.

Assignments

Pre-reading task

Before you read ... ➤ p. 18

Imagine you emigrate to another country. What would you miss most about your home country?

Apart from one's family and friends, students are likely to name the language and several cultural traditions typical of their home country.

Their ideas should be collected on the board, maybe as a mind-map or cluster, to serve as a reminder for the later discussion about home, cultural identity and national origin.

While-reading-task

p. 18

Why do people in Japan consider it polite to turn down an offer in the first place? Which cultural standard is responsible for that?

This convention is apparently based on an extreme idea of politeness as well as the intention not to appear too greedy. One's personal needs should remain in the background, only a repeated offer might lead the guest to express his or her wish. Modesty is the cultural value which is responsible for this behaviour.

Activities

Contrasts between the different cultures p. 18

Looking back on the chapter, point out the main different cultural differences (traditions, conventions, the role of the woman, etc.) between Japan, China and Vietnam on the one hand and the United States on the other. Find more examples.

The students are encouraged to recapitulate everything they have learnd about American and Asian culture respectively. The following cultural standards and values might be mentioned: individualism vs. sense of community, egotism vs. altruism, the fulfilment of one's personal needs as the highest ideal vs. modesty and religiousness; anonymity vs. socializing etc.

Personal experience p. 19

Think of cultural differences you have come across travelling abroad. Name some of the foreign manners, rituals, norms, rules, values and ceremonies that you found extremely strange. Explain your feelings.

The answer to this task depends on the students' individual experiences in foreign countries and therefore is difficult to predict. Their ideas of what is different or even strange might vary from foreign eating habits to differences in communication and the way people in other countries spend their free time, for example.

Discussing multi-ethnicity: the ideal way to integration, conformity or tolerance? p. 19

The question that often arises when one talks about people living in a foreign country is whether immigrants should adjust to the cultural standards of the country they live in and abandon their own cultural background or whether the original inhabitants have to tolerate the minority with its different culture.
Find arguments for both positions and prepare a panel discussion. Take this picture as a starting point.

This being the central issue associated with the idea of a multicultural society, it should be given enough time to be discussed in class. The students are sure to be familiar with this controversy since Germany is the home of many immigrants from different countries as well. There are advantages and disadvantages connected with both concepts, conformity as well as tolerance, and therefore the organization of a panel discussion, which should be prepared by the students themselves, appears to be the appropriate approach.

While every society requires a certain amount of assimilation of the immigrants so that co-existence can work peacefully, nobody can force people to give up their cultural and national roots. It is a fact that people who are forced to do so will suffer from their being *torn between two worlds* and might even become mentally ill. The ideal solution seems to be a mixture of the two concepts, the respective predominance of which has to be defined for each single part of society anew. Social fields worth discussing might be school, education, professional life, politics, for example.

Chapter 2: Im-Migrants – Needed But Not Wanted

Vorbemerkungen zum Kapitel

Befasste sich das erste Kapitel mit Lebensauffassungen, die *Asian-Americans* in der Auseinandersetzung mit ihren eigenen und den amerikanischen Werten und Normen entwickelt haben, stehen in diesem Kapitel die Wahrnehmungsweisen im Mittelpunkt, mit denen sich *white* und *Mexican-Americans* begegnen. Der erste Text führt aus mexikanischer Sicht exemplarisch in die Probleme und die Perspektiven der Integration ein. Zwei weitere Texte erlauben die nähere Auseinandersetzung mit dem Blick, mit dem die ansässig Gewordenen auf die Einwanderer und ihr Schicksal schauen. Dabei geht es immer auch um die Herausarbeitung der Werthaltungen und Wahrnehmungsmuster, die diesen Sichtweisen übergeordnet sind. Dementsprechend schließt das Kapitel mit einem Text ab, mit dem die Frage nach Offenheit und Abgrenzung in den Bereich menschliche Grunddispositionen zur Orientierung einerseits an der kollektiven sozialen Erfahrung, andererseits an der eigenen Beobachtung von Lebensvorgängen gerückt wird.

Start here

Distant neighbours p. 20

Different languages, different traditions, different values, but a common border: Look at this collection of stereotypes Americans and Mexicans have created for each other. Do you recognize parts of your own stock picture of Gringos and Latinos?

Die einführende Karikatur bietet sich an, klischeehafte Vorstellungen der weißen Amerikaner und der Mexikaner bzw. Latinos voneinander zunächst anhand der Bilder zu versprachlichen und dann unter Einbezug auch unserer eigenen Vorstellungen von diesen beiden Gruppen zu diskutieren. Anhand des Gegensatzes zwischen einer „Mañana-Mentality“ und einer „Time is Money-Mentality“ können die unterschiedlichen Wertvorstellungen, die diesen Haltungen unterliegen, in ihren positiven und negativen Seiten näher beschrieben werden. Einen weiteren Gesprächspunkt kann die Frage bilden, woher solche klischeehaften Vorstellungen kommen bzw. wie sie verbreitet werden.

Growing up in a Migrant Setting

Francisco Jiménez

Author

Now a distinguished scholar, teacher, writer and editor, Francisco Jiménez was born in Mexico in 1943. When he was 4, his family moved to California and at the age of 6 he began to work in the fields. Despite frequent moves and even deportation back to Mexico as an illegal alien, Jiménez pursued his education with determination. He became an American citizen and is now a full professor of Modern Languages and Literatures at Santa Clara University.

Synopsis of the text

A homodiegetic narration told from the perspective of a twelve year old boy (Panchito), "The Circuit" is about the life of a Mexican family as a part of the migrant workforce on Californian farms. When Panchito is allowed to go to school in November, his first experiences are marked by feelings of separation and difference, of frustration and anger at not being able to perform as he thinks he should. His teacher, Mr. Lema, proves to be very understanding and supportive and soon offers to teach Panchito to play the trumpet. Returning home all excited with this great news, Panchito, however, has to face the fact that his family is on the move again.

Unterrichtsempfehlungen

Vorbemerkungen
Der Text veranschaulicht Probleme der Verständigung, die das Leben in einer fremden Kultur mit sich bringt, durch Figurenkreis (mexikanische Wanderarbeiter), Fokalisierung (Perspektive des lernwilligen Schuljungen) und das offene Ende: der Freude des Jungen über die Möglichkeit, in der Fremde mit dem Erlernen des Trompetespielens auch die eigene kulturelle Identität zum Ausdruck bringen zu können, wird durch den Wegzug der Familie sogleich wieder die konkrete Perspektive genommen.

1. Schwerpunkt
Die positive Haltung des mexikanischen Jungen zum Schulbesuch sollte im Vergleich mit den Ansichten der Lerngruppe herausgearbeitet werden (Meinungsumfrage/Kartenabfrage zum Bild der Schule allgemein oder zur Schule als Ort, um für ein besseres Leben zu lernen).

2. Schwerpunkt
Ausgehend von der genaueren Erarbeitung der Erfahrungen des Jungen und ihrer Bedeutung für ihn sollte der erschwerte Zugang zu Ausbildung und Kultur (Sprache) einerseits als Ursachen- und Folgenkreis deprivierter Lebensmöglichkeiten, andererseits aber auch als Auslöser zielgerichteten Strebens thematisiert werden.
Zur Vertiefung auch durch den Vergleich zwischen homodiegetischer Erzählung und Autorenbiografie empfiehlt es sich, eine Biografie von Francisco Jiménez hinzuzuziehen, die mit Zusatzinformationen zu Jiménez über die Web-Seiten der Santa Clara University angeboten wird:

http://www.scu.edu/SCU/Departments/ModernLanguages/deptdir.html
bzw. http://www.scu.edu/SCU/Programs/Diversity/frjm.html

Assignments

Pre-reading task

Crossing the border, looking for work p. 21

Look at the map of California and name chief areas of agricultural production. Can you sketch routes a Mexican migrant worker and his family might follow from spring to late fall?

Chief areas of agricultural production: San Joaquin and Sacramento Valley; Mexican migrant workers would move within this region of about 300 miles N->S (Sacramento, Stockton, Modesto, Merced, Fresno, Visalja, Bakersfield), but also go to or come from e.g. Imperial Valley, the coast (Santa Barbara) and Napa Valley. Migrant workers might of course find seasonal labour in other branches of industry, too, e.g. the service sector in recreational areas.

While-reading tasks

p. 21

Separation and difference – explain how these words sum up the experiences this day holds in store for the boy.

Separation: His father and his brother go to pick cotton; in the school bus he sits in an empty seat in the back.
Difference: His brother cannot go to school and is sad; all the other pupils carry books; he has missed a good part of the term and has to enroll before he can enter his class; the language that comes naturally to him is Spanish; his command of English is poor; he cannot perform in class.
Separation/Isolation: It will be difficult for him to share this day's experiences and emotions with someone who simply understands.

p. 23

Mr. Lema and the trumpet – what does this mean to the migrant boy from Mexico?

Mr. Lema proves to be a very understanding teacher; the sound of the trumpet puts the boy into contact with his native culture; learning to play the trumpet is a way of expressing his native culture and a key to the universal language of music; experiences of separation and difference yield to expectations of integration and communication (cf. the prestige of membership in a school band in the U.S.).

p. 23

Imagine: What goes on in the boy's mind when he sees the cardboard boxes?

It dawns on him that his family is going to move again. His emotional response is possibly marked by feelings of shock, disbelief, anger, frustration, helplessness, subjection.

Activities

Biographical influences on and in literature p. 24

1. "I don't even get a chance to say good-bye to Mr. Lema" could well be one of the thoughts that crossed the protagonist's mind when he saw the cardboard boxes. Later, however, he may have found time to write a farewell letter to Mr. Lema. Think about various possibilities regarding purpose, content and style and then write this letter for him.

Purpose: say good-bye, farewell; express his gratitude; explain why he won't come to Mr. Lema's class any more; confide his feelings; complain about the situation he is in; ask for help …
Contents: his life in a migrant family; his experiences at school; his special relationship to Mr. Lema; the open future …
Style: matter of fact and loyal to his family; warm and friendly; marked by anger and frustration …

2. Francisco Jiménez chose "The Circuit" as the title for the short story from which the excerpt above is taken. What does this title add to your understanding of the excerpt?

It can be seen as a reference to the pattern of harvests which dictates the places where the boy and his family live and work at throughout the year. Since this nomadic life turns the boy's education and integration into a series of starts and stops, a more general significance can be attributed to the events in the story: migrant workers and their families are forever running in a circuit (are trapped in a vicious circle) of poverty, poor education, rootlessness and little if any integration into society and culture at large.

3. "The Circuit" first appeared in print in *The Arizona Quarterly* in 1973. Twenty years later the story was included in an anthology called *Growing up Chicana/o. Stories of the joys, pains, frustrations and triumphs of a Mexican-American childhood*. What purpose could there be to publish such an anthology?

Its purpose is to make the Mexican-American (Chicana/o) voices heard among the many voices of American society. By calling attention to its formative years, the anthology both claims and substantiates the idea of an unmistakable Chicana/o identity. Stories on growing up bring an important and probably yet undocumented part of the past of the Chicanas/os back to life, help us to understand their present situation and provide signposts to chart a course for the future. For the present generation of Chicanas/os the anthology fills a void because they can relate to these stories much better than to the stories about what it means to grow up in white America. For the American society as a whole, the anthology is an invitation to come to a better understanding of one of its parts and to recognize and appreciate the contributions Chicanas/os have already made and will be able to make to America.

4. Francisco Jiménez has become a man of letters, working as a teacher, professor, writer and editor of bilingual magazines. What do you think: are Francisco Jiménez' professional activities a reflection of his childhood experiences? Use this as a

starting point for a more general discussion: How important are the experiences we make as we grow up for what we choose to do later in our lives?

As in the case of Francisco Jiménez, experiences of loss and deprivation and encounters with positive role models one makes while growing up may well stimulate strong desires regarding one's own future. They also play an important part in the provision of the sometimes tremendous amount of energy that it takes to turn these desires into reality. Still, our growing-up years should not be seen as the only ones in which key experiences are possibly exerting an influence upon the course of our lives and maybe even change it altogether. While Jiménez' biography certainly belies the more general significance that can be attributed to the title of his short story, the fact that he chose this title may be understood as a true-to-life comment that our experiences, however deeply they are felt, cannot always work against the conditions (and, what needs to be added here, traditions) we live in. Students may also be encouraged to discuss whether a limited number of clear-cut impressions and choices is more helpful to find one's way and place in life than a perhaps overwhelming abundance of possible experiences and choices. There is yet another dimension to this question if one discusses the nature and amount of our choices not only with respect to our social and cultural environment, but also with respect to our genetic endowment.

Plane Wreck at Los Gatos

Woody Guthrie, Martin Hoffmann

Author

Woody Guthrie (1912–1967), popular and influential American songwriter and folk musician. His main achievement is seen in the way he turned the folk ballad into a vehicle for social protest. His sympathy for the downtrodden is based on the experiences he made among hobos and dustbowl refugees in the 1930s. More information can be found on the WWW (cf. activity 1).

Synopsis of the text

Inspired by an incident in January 1948, the song is a biting criticism of the way Mexican seasonal labourers are treated by Americans, particularly as regards deportation practices of the 1950s. With overtones of death and decay, the end of a harvest season with its consequences for the Mexican workers is sketched in stanza 1. Stanzas 2–4 describe the life of migrant workers from a Mexican point of view. The song culminates in stanzas 5 and 6 with the report of the plane crash and a number of sharp and pointed questions which are levelled at the Americans by what can be interpreted as the voice of America herself.

Unterrichts-empfehlungen

Vorbemerkungen
Über die Stichworte „corridos/ballads“ kann unmittelbar an den vorhergehenden Text angeknüpft werden (evt. Aktivierung des Vorwissens zu „ballads“ und spätere Vertiefung am Text in activity 3 oder auch Präsentation von „La cucaracha“ als bekanntestem Beispiel eines corrido) und Guthries Aussage zum Zweck seiner Lieder diskutiert werden. Inhaltlich und thematisch werden Deportationen nicht nur als eine weitere Seite des Lebens mexikanischer Wanderarbeiter in den Vereinigten Staaten sichtbar, sondern auch als ein Ansatzpunkt amerikanischer Sozialkritik.

1. Schwerpunkt
Eigenständige inhaltliche Erarbeitung des Textes mit Hilfe des WWW.

2. Schwerpunkt
Analyse und kritische Auseinandersetzung mit der Art und Weise, wie hier Sozialkritik als Engagement für eine im eigenen Land fremde und ausgebeutete Gruppe vorgetragen wird.

Assignments

Pre-reading task

Speaking for the underprivileged p. 24

An old-fashioned statement on the purpose of popular music?

It states the intention of changing American society for the better and also the belief/hope that a song can actually do that (G. a forerunner of protest-singers). It is an example of American positive thinking and illustrates the influence of the media industry on public life in the US.

Activities

More than just the music p. 25–26

1. To fully understand this song, you need to know more than just the vocabulary. Take verses 4 and 9 as an example and find out how a map of Mexico and the United States can help you to a better understanding. More background information on this song is offered in the *World Wide Web*. Find out those pieces of information which improve your understanding of the song and report them to your class. Making use of the *World Wide Web*, you may even want to prepare a little presentation on Woody Guthrie.

Verses 4, 9: Wading the Rio Grande is one of the ways illegal immigrants from Mexico choose to get into the U.S. – hence their derogatory name *wetbacks*. *Braceros*, on the other hand, are seasonal workers with a legal status. They came to the U.S. in particularly large numbers on contract labor programs which were set up between Mexico and the U.S. between 1942 and 1964, at first as a direct response to the labor shortage caused by World War II (cf ll. 13/14).
WWW-activity: Depending on their expertise, students can start working on this activity straight away or they will have to find out

first, by way of a general introduction, how to obtain the required information from the www (probably the best strategy is to use a search engine and enter the more complete title of the song, "Plane Wreck at Los Gatos", as a phrase, but students should rather be encouraged to follow their own strategies and report on their effectiveness).
There are a number of websites which offer the lyrics of the song, sometimes in slightly different versions. Information on the song and its historical background (deportation policies of the '50s, the plane crash, the practice of dumping citrus crops) has been incorporated into some pages, e.g.:
http://www.geocities.com/Nashville/3448/deportee.html#aaa.
This page also offers a link to a www-music store which allows students to find out about records on which "Plane Wreck at Los Gatos" is performed (cf. among others, J. Cash/W. Jennings/K. Kristofferson/W. Nelson, *Highwayman* (Sony Music 1985) or the debut record of Latin pop group *Los Super Seven* (BMG/RCA 1998). For a short biography of Woody Guthrie, cf. the Rock'n Roll Hall of Fame: http://rockhall.com/induct/guthwood.html).
The best web-coverage of Woody Guthrie is offered with exemplary maintenance by David Arkush. For reliable access, enter "Woody Guthrie Pages" in a search engine.

2. You will have noticed that there is more than one language used in this song and that there is more than one speaker voicing the verses. Study this in more detail and give an explanation of the overall effect.

While stanzas 2–4 can quite obviously be attributed to a Mexican speaker, the chorus and stanzas 1, 5 and 6 require closer examination. The key to the identification of the speaker is to be found in the use of personal pronouns. As in stanza 4, Americans are refererred to as "you" in stanza 1. Still, the speaker cannot be identified as a Mexican since Mexicans are referred to as "them" in this stanza. A possible solution is to identify the speaker as an American who addresses his fellow citizens with a critical attitude. While stanza 5 may well be understood in the light of this identification, stanza 6 calls for a modification: it is impossible to attribute verse 27 to an American. What is heard here is rather the voice of America herself. In the chorus, this voice is of course able to directly address the Mexicans in their own language and by their names, thus setting herself apart from the Americans who lump all the individual Mexican migrant workers together as *deportees*.
Making the voice of America herself heard in this song creates the greatest authority possible for the sharp criticism of American behaviour which the song intends to make. The Americans are spoiling the beauty of their very land, are treating the values and ideals upon which it is built with disrespect. The true America is capable of embracing Mexican migrant workers as friends. The use of simple Spanish to address the Mexicans as individuals and the position of stanzas 2-4 in the middle of the poem support the idea of sympathy and integration as the proper alternative to common cold-hearted deportation practices.

3. Consult a dictionary of literary terms and find out about the ballad and its typical elements. Then apply your findings to "Plane Wreck at Los Gatos".

ballad: poem in short stanzas narrating a story, often concerned with the historical, heroic, marvellous and sentimental, rooted in folklore, marked by simplicity, dialogical elements, strong ties with musical performance.
All these elements apply to *Plane Wreck at Los Gatos*. The contents may be described as historical with a touch of the sentimental, with the open and pointed social criticism of course being a distinguishing mark of this song.

4. Remember: the young migrant boy from Mexico in "The Circuit" says that he likes "corridos" (ballads). What do you think: would he approve of "Plane Wreck at Los Gatos" as a good way to make Americans aware of the plight of Mexican migrant workers? Do you?

Points for discussion: the ballad leaves no doubt about its sympathies and criticism; it is targeted mainly at an American audience; it appeals to the core of American values, identity and national pride; as a popular form it may reach a wider audience; the criticism is tarnished by a hidden sentimentality and the use of a popular form that is meant to answer emotional needs, but not to stir to action; the Mexicans are shown as exploited and helpless victims with no choice of their own; Mexico is presented as a country that obviously has little if anything to offer to nourish her people; it is not a Mexican voice, but the voice of America and her values that the listener is supposed to identify with.

They're Mexicans – Bad for Business

T. Coraghessan Boyle

Author cf p. 23

Synopsis of the text

Kyra Menaker-Mossbacher, a successful real estate agent, is on her way to a customer's property when her attention is drawn to a group of Mexicans who have gathered next to the parking lot of a supermarket. The group is bigger than it used to be, and Kyra's professional eye immediately calculates the effect of this change on potential real-estate customers. Kyra decides to investigate further into this, interviews the employees of the supermarket and inspects the condition of the surrounding apartment buildings. Though she has to acknowledge that the process of deterioration which she observes in this and similar neighbourhoods has so far been good for her own professional success, an uneasy feeling grows within her that the increasing number of Mexicans might eventually spoil the real estate business in areas she deals with. She concludes that something must be done to prevent such a development. Returning to her car, she is addressed by one of the Mexicans.

Unterrichtsempfehlungen

Vorbemerkungen
Waren die beiden vorhergehenden Texte historisch in den 50er-Jahren angesiedelt, erfolgt mit diesem Auszug aus T.C. Boyle's Roman *The Tortilla Curtain* der Sprung in eine unmittelbare urbane Gegenwart der 90er-Jahre. Konkretisiert in zwei Paaren, präsentiert Boyles Roman in wechselnder Perspektivierung die Sicht mexikanischer Einwanderer und die eines sich von diesen praktisch belagert fühlenden gehobenen weißen Mittelstandes, der meint, seine soziale und kulturelle Rettung in Forderungen nach vollkommener Abschottung suchen zu müssen. Der heterodiegetisch erzählte Romanauszug bietet sich aufgrund seiner Fokalisierung durch die Figur der Kyra dazu an, diese Befindlichkeit an einem exemplarischen Fall etwas genauer zu betrachten. Mit einem Blick auf aktuelle demographische Prognosen und die Geschichte des amerikanischen Südwestens mit seiner ursprünglich spanischen Prägung lässt sich dann ein Kontext für die kritische Auseinandersetzung mit den Befürchtungen schaffen, die von weißen Amerikanern hinsichtlich einer kulturellen Überfremdung/eines Bedeutungsverlustes verspürt werden.

1. Schwerpunkt
Analytische und kreative Erarbeitung des Romanauszuges.

2. Schwerpunkt
Erarbeitung von Hintergrundwissen zur kritischen Auseinandersetzung mit der Festungsmentalität, die sich unter weißen Amerikanern in den Südweststaaten herausgebildet hat.

Hinweis
Zu Boyles Roman *The Tortilla Curtain* ist in der Reihe „EinFach Englisch" im Programm des Verlags F. Schöningh ein Unterrichtsmodell erschienen (Best.-Nr. 41203-5).

Assignments

Pre-reading task

Think before you read p. 26

Students should freely comment on the picture and the excerpt from a brochure which are juxtaposed here.
What kind of people are shown in the picture and are addressed by the brochure? What emotions are evoked and appealed to? Would you like to live at Fox Fire Estates and why (not)? What kind of relation can be established between the two items – simple contrast (poor vs. rich and perhaps a widening gap between the two), cause and effect (the brochure answers a feeling of being disturbed, maybe even threatened by the people shown in the picture). What are the consequences if these are two sides of the same society.

While-reading-tasks

p. 28 ➤ What does Kyra probably think of this conversation?

In this conversation, Kyra has not gained any information at all. She may think that the Asian woman in the store is not really aware of the situation the store is in, that her command of English is too poor to talk about this, that she simply does not care becauese she is only an employee or because she has, after all, an immigrant background herself.

p. 28 ➤ Why does Kyra keep her gaze fixed on the row of cheap apartments?

She assumes that the Mexicans would take any kind of eye-contact as an invitation to address her.

p. 28 ➤ "Schools, that's what it was all about." – Explain.

One of the pull-factors that attract immigrants from Mexico to American cities are schools and the American educational system since this is a promise of a better future for the next generation. If school busses do not operate in the county, this attraction, however, is lost.

Activities

Working on a character p. 29 ➤ The events in this passage are clearly seen through Kyra's eyes. Give some examples which make this particularly evident and then write a sketch of Kyra's character as it is revealed in this passage.

The fact that the descriptions of the Mexicans and of the neighbourhood are presented with all the observations a professional real estate agent is likely to make is the most obvious clue that the passage is seen through Kyra's eyes. As there are some clear cases of reported thought/interior monologue (cf. 16/17, 18; 30, 56–60), reflections such as what the situation would be like in Tijuana (cf. 39–43) or what the future of real estate business might look like (73–75) should also rather be attributed to Kyra than understood as a comment of the narrator.
Kyra's character appears to be mainly built upon her professional existence as a real estate agent. She appears to be self-confident and straight-forward and not at all hesitant or anxious to look more closely at a matter of business even if this involves her in a situation which may become unpleasant. Yet, she entertains a number of prejudices and a shallow tolerance which can limit her opportunities both in life and in business. It is also possible to detect a craving for simple solutions: she calls for strong action against the Mexicans, but at the same time she does not really know what this means in practice and prefers to leave this for others to decide.

Acting out the climax p. 29 ➤ The excerpt ends with a close contact between a female white American and a male Mexican. Work in a team: first create a still shot of the scene, then write down how it may develop in the form of a screenplay. Prepare to give a presentation in class.

In performing this activity, students have to find answers to a number of questions, such as: does the Mexican approach Kyra in a modest or a demanding way (cf. ll. 39–56)? How does Kyra respond, bearing in mind that she is, in principle, in search of a strong answer to the situation (cf. ll. 61–64)? Do the other Mexicans keep their distance or will they get involved in some way or other? Is the situation bound for an explosion of resentment, frustration and hate? Are there chances for communication and understanding? Or will the situation develop in a way that is marked by the completely unspectacular? Each presentation should be discussed with respect to underlying assumptions regarding the behaviour of the characters and the development of a situation of dormant intercultural conflict.

1. *Tortilla Curtain*, the title of Boyle's novel, is a name that has been given to the Mexican-American border. Due to the increasing deployment of the most modern of border control technology, this border has also been called *Silicon Wall*. Explain the idea behind these two metaphors and comment.

Placing the text in a wider context p. 29

Tortilla Curtain – a combination of references to Mexican food and the Iron Curtain of the Cold War period; *Silicon Wall* – a combination of references to Silicon Valley and the Berlin Wall. Whether seriously intended or not, both metaphors thus establish a comparison between the Mexican-American border and the boundary line between political, social and economic systems such as the East and the West in Europe in the the wake of World War II. Whereas this boundary line was chiefly drawn on ideological grounds, the Mexican-American border can hardly be associated with ideological, but rather with economical and, from the perspective particularly of white Americans, ethnic and cultural differences. A point deserving further discussion is the effect that is created with the choice of these two metaphors: simply a pun; a comment with particular criticism of the Americans (cf. their role in the conflict between East and West); a hint at the possible basis of major conflicts after the age of ideologies seems to have come to an end.
A note on the illustration: the illustration is taken from Jack Kurtz' permanent WWW-Photo Gallery "The Tortilla Curtain" (http://home.att.net/~jackkurtz/contents.html). As an extra activity, students could have a closer look at this exhibition and write a review. Jack Kurtz has kindly agreed to try and answer students' e-mails with questions on the Mexican-American border and his work.

2. *Coming Home?* Prepare a report on the events that shaped the Mexican-American border in the 19th century. Then discuss whether it is fair to say that Mexican immigrants to California are resettling land they once owned.

The material offered on pages 29–30 is to inspire students to discuss the social, political and cultural effects of the growing number of Hispanics in the Californian/American population and to make their own investigations into the history of the southwestern states of America. This involves research on the role of Spain in the colonization of America and on the Mexican-American War with its consequences. The question for discussion is put in a provocative way to make students aware of the fact that common perceptions of ethnic change in the American Southwest are often tinged with unquestioned concepts of white American historiography or of an America that owes its true existence and identity almost exclusively to the contributions of those who came there from Western Europe.

Mending Wall Robert Frost

Author

Robert Lee Frost (1874-1963) gained first recognition for his poetry during the three years he spent in England between 1912 and 1915. Back in the United States at the age of 41, he became an established poet and taught literature at various universities while living on farms in Vermont and New Hampshire. The life and scenery of rural New England, the idiom and the values of this region have exerted a strong influence on his poetry which shows a wide and deep emotional range and in its ordinary subject matter often reflects one of the major themes in American literature, the conflict between nature/innocence and human society/experience.

Synopsis of the text

Almost an anecdote, the poem is about two neighbours who meet in spring to mend the wall that separates their estates. The person speaking appears to be the younger of the two, and the poem presents his observations and reflections on the point and purpose of boundary lines, establishing a contrast betwen the way life and nature work against walls and make them appear as altogether useless and the older neighbour's insistence on the proverbial social good of walls and fences.

Unterrichtsempfehlungen

Vorbemerkungen
Nach der Auseinandersetzung mit der gegenwärtigen Diskussion um das Zusammenleben im amerikanisch-mexikanischen Grenzraum kann Frosts Gedicht dazu anregen, sich mit den konträren Ansichten einer grundsätzlich auf Begegnung angelegten Natur des Menschen und einer aus der Erfahrung zwischenmenschlicher Konflikte erwachsenen Zurückhaltung und Abgrenzung auseinander zu setzen. Gleichberechtigt neben einem solchen Umgang mit dem Text als Anknüpfungspunkt für eine grundsätzliche Diskussion über Werte und Haltungen, denen interkulturelle Begegnungen unterliegen können, steht jedoch seine Würdigung als literarisches Kunstwerk.

1. Schwerpunkt
Interpretation des Textes und Auseinandersetzung mit den Grenzen der Interpretation.

2. Schwerpunkt
Aufgreifen einer Textinterpretation als Grundlage einer Debatte über das Pro und Contra von Ab- bzw. Eingrenzung.

Assignments

Activities

1. Robert Frost's poem rests upon a contradiction. Identify the verses which most clearly state this contradiction, characterize the two positions involved in greater detail and comment on the significance of verse 23.

From appreciation to interpretation p. 32

The poem is built upon a contradiction between two opposing views on border walls. This is made particularly obvious by the fact that the two positions are juxtaposed in the first and the last verse of the poem. The first verse is a general statement that can be attributed to the younger neighbour. It is supported by many observations which culminate in his vain effort to identify more exactly what it is that does not love a wall. The last verse is a proverb which the younger neighbour quotes from the older. Already introduced in verse 27, the proverb clearly and unmistakably maintains the principal value of boundary lines.
Since the critical view of border walls is attributed to the younger neighbour who is the person speaking in the poem, this view pervades the poem. To the younger neighbour, the effort of maintaining border walls is at best "just another kind of outdoor game" (21), the wall itself as much an object of playful ridicule (24–26) as of critical questioning (32–35). The younger neighbour's view is based on the observations of an individual and innocent eye which simply records the futility of maintaining border walls against what it perceives to be the natural course of things (1–11, 15–20) and a challenging mind which even suspects an earlier, less civilized and enlightened state of mind in the insistence upon border walls (38–42).
Though basically limited to its proverbial expression in verses 27 and 45, the positive view of border walls which is attributed to the older neighbour maintains its ground as a clear, simple and solid expression of a wisdom based on collective rather than individual experience that man cannot live contentedly and peacefully without walls, boundaries, limits and self-limitations. Characteristic of this position is the clarity and simpliciy of its expression which sets it apart from the more witty, albeit at times somewhat evasive (cf. 35–38) presentation of its counterpart and which may well be the reason why it succeeds in gaining the momentum to claim the last line of the poem with an air of apparently untarnished authority.
Verse 23 splits the poem into two halves of 22 verses. It marks a transition between the two halves since it can both be read as a conclusion of the younger neighbour's individual observations on border walls and as an opening to the argument he is having with the older neighbour resp. with the collective wisdom puts forth by him.

2. Robert Frost is often praised for the conversational tone he built into his verse and the way he attributes universal significance to what could be mere anecdotes. Show how this poem is a good example of these qualities.

The language of the poem bears traits of oral language use and communication; an element of dialogue becomes prominent particularly in its second half; the poem is built upon what appears to be an authentic scene from rural New England; it is concerned with witty observations and proverbial wisdom; it has few if any references to bookish learning. A general, symbolic meaning lies in the topical choice (Mending Wall) and its dialogical presentation, in particular with the questions of the younger neighbour (31/32) and the two suggestions that there are basic forces of life which are opposed to walls (35–38) and that an insistence upon the good of walls is a sign of a more primitive state of mind (38-42).

3. Name the two examples Untermeyer gives of an interpretation of "Mending Wall".
   How do you understand the reference to the "poet himself" and his insistence that the poem does not say more than it seems to say? A rebuttal of any interpretative effort – discuss.

A straightforward interpretation resting on a topical *pars pro toto* approach places the poem in the context of a discussion on the point of national boundaries; a symbolic interpretation focusing on the two neighbours sees them as representatives of two basic human attitudes, the spirit of revolt and progress and the spirit of restraint and tradition. *Points for discussion:* A poet has to reject efforts to attribute a single meaning to one of his creations because it limits the creative freedom of the recipient whose understanding constitutes meaning and thus is a legitimate interpretation of the work. A poem such as Frost's comes truly alive only in our discussion of what "it seems to say" – which, after all, is already a matter of debate.

Organizing a classroom-debate **p. 32**

Imagine that one day the two neighbours start to argue about the purpose of border walls. You might start with another look at the picture on p. 29. Then give examples from different walks of life which each of them might use to support his view. You may want to make this question the topic of a formal debate in your classroom: take a poll first, then have two parties advocate the two positions before the rest of the class. The two parties present their arguments in a brief statement and are questioned by an audience. Take another poll after the debate to see if some of you changed your minds. If you want to turn this into a proper exercise in debating, some of you will have to observe and afterwards comment on the presentation of arguments and the response of and to the audience.

Possible references: border walls in history and today; the frontier as an American topic, border lines as a means of segregation, confinement or protection; border lines and boundaries as a means of orientation and organization (geography, society, culture, identity, responsibilty, stages in life, …); border lines as an incentive for / an impediment to innovation and change; border lines as a correlate to limited resources and capacities (not only material, but also with a view to limits of human understanding and sympathy); border lines as an obstacle on the way to a brotherhood of man.
With its discussion on the need to close the U.S.-Mexican border, chapter 7 in Boyle's *Tortilla Curtain* offers another starting point for the debate proposed in this activity.

Chapter 3:

The Limits of Mutual Understanding

Vorbemerkungen zum Kapitel

Dieses Kapitel ist ein für deutsche Schülerinnen und Schüler sehr sensibles Kapitel, so wie insgesamt das Sprechen über das Grauen der Naziherrschaft und vor allem über den *holocaust* Einfühlungsvermögen fordert, um nicht das Gegenteil der beabsichtigten Wirkung auszulösen, nämlich Abwehr und Überdruss.
Im thematischen Zusammenhang dieses Heftes geht es vor allem darum, dass die hier vorgestellten Schicksale von Juden – Einzelne und Familien, Personen der Zeit- und Wissenschaftsgeschichte oder literarische Fiktionen – anders noch als die in den vorangegangenen Kapiteln dargestellten Emigranten und Immigranten, Opfer einer auf ihre Auslöschung ausgerichteten Ideologie waren, die ihren Neuanfang in der fremden Welt nicht nur zu einem Akt der Befreiung sondern der Erlösung machte. Manche radikale Weigerung jüdischer Exilanten, je wieder Deutschland zu besuchen oder die deutsche Sprache zu gebrauchen (vgl. dazu Bernard Malamud, „The German Refugee“ in *Imagining America*, hg. von Wesley Brown und Amy Ling) wird aus dieser Erfahrung verständlich. Und doch zeigen die hier gewählten Beispiele, absolut typisch, den Grad der Verwurzeltheit gerade der jüdischen Intellektuellen in der Kultur und dem Geist, vor deren schrecklichster Manifestation sie geflohen waren. Insofern spiegeln die Lebensläufe das Bewusstsein der meisten Exilanten, Wanderer zwischen zwei Welten zu sein.
Angesichts der Unvorstellbarkeit und auch Unvergleichbarkeit dieser Verfolgung und Vernichtung wird man, spätestens bei Art Spiegelmans *Maus,* die Frage nach den Möglichkeiten der Kunst und Literatur, das Gedenken wach zu halten und der Wiederholung zu wehren, stellen müssen. Auf die nicht nur für das amerikanische Judentum in seiner Identität und Existenz schicksalhafte Bedeutung dieser Erinnerungskultur hat zuletzt Peter Novick in *The Holocaust in American Life* hingewiesen. Bei der Frage, was Literatur denn über Faktensammlung und Geschichtsschreibung hinaus vermag, sollte man auch den Film einbeziehen, so z.B. Steven Spielbergs *Schindler's List.*

Start here

Auto- and heterostereotypes p. 33

Der einführende Text verweist auf zwei bedeutende deutschstämmige jüdische Emigranten, auf Kurt Lewin und Albert Einstein. Zu beiden sollten die Schüler Informationen einholen. Nähere Hinweise auf Lewins Beitrag zur Kulturpsychologie und zum Selbst- und Fremdbild von Deutschen und Amerikanern finden sich bei Alexander Tho-

mas und Karl Heinz Wagner, „Von der Fremdheitserfahrung zum interkulturellen Verstehen“, PRAXIS 46 (1999) 3, S. 227–236. Die Lernenden dürften begreifen, dass jüdische Exilanten wie keine andere Gruppe vor oder nach ihnen, tragischerweise dazu prädestiniert waren, über Selbst- und Fremdbilder zu reflektieren und sich darauf einzustellen, nicht zuletzt als Teil einer Überlebensstrategie.
Anregung zu einer Untersuchungsaufgabe: Kurzbiografie zu Albert Einstein, Thomas Mann, Bertolt Brecht; Hinweise zu einer anregenden Präsentation (unter Einbeziehung von Medien und Anschauungsmaterialien, *handouts*) im Kurs.

Life in exile ➤ p. 33

Look at the portraits of these men. Find out who they are, what made them leave their native Germany. What did they do in the States, where did they live? Find out more about what living in the New World felt like for them.
Collecting dates and keywords; think of their motives for emigrating. Imagine what life in exile meant for them.

Konzentration auf das Problem: *What does living in another country, i. e. being a stranger in a foreign country mean?*; Blicklenkung auf Aspekte der Sozialisation und Enkulturation; Fortführung mit Hinweisen auf die Biografien von Thomas Mann und Bertolt Brecht, die, noch anders als die Wissenschaftler Einstein und Lewin, sozusagen von ihrer (Mutter)Sprache, von der durch die Sprache gestifteten Gemeinschaft von Autor und Leser lebten (Heimatlosigkeit des Exildichters).

The Americans and the Europeans – My First Impressions Albert Einstein

Author

Albert Einstein was born in Ulm (Germany) in 1879 and taught physics at the universities of Prague and Zürich before he became the Director of the Kaiser-Wilhelm-Institut für Physik in Berlin from 1914 until 1933 when he was forced by the Nazis to leave Germany. He then taught at Princeton, N. J. where he died in 1955. His work revolutionized the theory of modern physics and made him the greatest scientific authority of the 20th century; he was awarded the Nobel Prize in 1921.

Synopsis of the text

First impressions, quite impressive; definition of the American national character in comparison with European (and Asian) national traits and cultural and civilizational achievements; all in all a very positive view of American society and the American people though not blind to their shortcomings (for details: see under *While reading tasks*).

Unterrichts-empfehlungen

Vorbemerkungen
Die Hinführung zum Text sollte speziell auf das Datum und die Umstände der Publikation abheben: 1921, drei Jahre nach dem Great War, dem 1. Weltkrieg, im Gefolge der Verleihung des Nobelpreises für Physik äußert sich Einstein in einer niederländischen Zeitung über Amerikaner und Europäer. Man vergegenwärtige sich die ungeheure wissenschaftliche und moralische Autorität dieses Deutschen, auf den die Welt hört.

1. Schwerpunkt
Die Klarheit und Schlüssigkeit der Argumentation sollte durch Strukturierung des Textes und Nachzeichnen des Argumentationsaufbaus nachvollzogen werden.

2. Schwerpunkt
Ein zweiter Schwerpunkt ist die Auflistung der Beobachtungen im Vergleich von Amerikanern, Europäern und Asiaten (in Spalten) und die Begründung der aus den Beobachtungen abgeleiteten Schlussfolgerungen.

3. Schwerpunkt
Unter dem Stichwort der Globalisierung sind die Kontinente und Länder enger zusammen gerückt. Wie weit schränkt das die Geltung von Einsteins Eindrücken und Folgerungen ein? Vergleich der eigenen Vorstellungen mit denen Einsteins.

Assignments

Pre-reading task

Before you read … p. 34

Think before you read: "… a Jew who regards other Jews as his brothers." (Einstein about himself)

Expression of brotherhood, of loyalty and of responsibility for his fellow-Jews and a reason for his later conflict with the Nazis in which he took the side of the Jews.

While-reading tasks

p. 34

Fundamental contrasts between Americans and Europeans according to Einstein. Name some.

Superiority in technology and organization, saving human labor; joyous, positive attitude towards life, friendly nature of people, agreeable intercourse with them; primary importance of material comforts of life; emphasis on the "we" which accounts for American economic superiority; contrary to this "social sense" relative restriction of the role of the State; extremely unequal distribution of property but no intolerable hardship because of the social conscience of the well-to-do; enormous influence of public opinion; lowering of the prestige of government (especially because of Prohibition) which in turn also accounts for the lack of people exchanging their views; therefore greater influence of the Press; scientific achievements in America; America's great responsibility as the leading world power.

p. 34

Make a list of the various traits of the American national character Einstein mentions.

List: technology- and organization-minded, joyous and positive, friendly, self-confident, optimistic, without envy; materialistic, concerned about comforts of life; future-oriented; not much of an individualist, trend towards conformity; cooperative, feels socially responsible, community-minded; critical of state interference; dependent on the press and public opinion; advanced in science; people in general not interested in international affairs; the nation not yet fully aware of its decisive role in international politics.

p. 35

In addition to the role of the individual, what does Einstein have to say about government and society?

Activities of the State (especially those of the central government) are restricted, many initiatives are in private hands; even the distribution of wealth (a key issue of the social welfare state) is left to private initiative and cultural functions (schools, universities, museums) are left to private enterprise because of the highly developed social conscience of the well-to-do. On the other hand, the prestige of the government has been lowered (Prohibition, a law that cannot be enforced and leads to double standards and to rising crime).

p. 35

Explore Einstein's view on the influence of the press.

Einstein sees the enormous influence of the Press in the States which is partly a result of the size of the country in which due to the distances communication through the media has taken the place of a more personal exchange of views and ideas (e.g. in public houses). Nowadays, with the worldwide web and at least one radio and one TV set in every household, communication has become even more depersonalized and the danger of manipulation even more dramatic.

Activities

Timeless attitudes? p. 36

1. Nicolas Bentley drew this picture in 1948. State what situation it shows.

Quite obviously, Einstein has been invited to address a wider audience (cf. microphone) or to speak over the radio, probably on some scientific topic.

2. How does he portray the different attitudes and reactions?

Einstein is formally dressed, has his notes in his hands, seems a little introverted and to feel out of place. His host, almost towering over him, is extremely relaxed and jovial and broadly grinning. He gives his guest an encouraging pat on the back, which makes Einstein's hair stand on end. Black and white technique together with the distorted proportions are meant to underline the discrepancy between the American and European way of life, also the discrepancy between the seriousness of the scientist's work and what we would now call infotainment. To some extent, the cartoon also throws light on the Englishman's idea of how Einstein should be treated in public. Remember: All this was drawn more than fifty years ago and appeared in George Mikes's *How to Scrape Skies*, a satirical view of the United States.

Say This City Has Ten Million Souls Wystan Hugh Auden

Author

Wystan Hugh Auden (1907–1973), influential English poet, closely linked with Germany, especially Berlin, where he lived from time to time. He took an active part in politics, held left wing views partly reflected in the engaged and didactic poetry of his younger years. He lived in the United States during the war, became a US citizen in 1946 but later returned to England to become Professor of Poetry at Oxford University.

Synopsis of the text

The twelve stanzas of the narrative poem tell the story of a German-Jewish couple trying to emigrate. They have no home anymore, and wherever they ask for shelter and protection they are rejected. In the end they become the helpless victims of Hitler's soldiers who persecute them.

Unterrichtsempfehlungen

Vorbemerkungen
Das Gedicht soll einstimmen in eine Thematik, die wenig an Aktualität verloren hat: die Verfolgung und Vertreibung von Menschen aus politischen, ethnischen oder religiösen Gründen. Erst die internationale Solidarität der demokratischen Staaten hat das Schicksal der Betroffenen gelindert, wenn sie auch oft genug Mord, Vergewaltigung und Vertreibung nicht verhindern konnte. Vor diesem Hintergrund stellt sich die Frage nach Vorurteil oder gar Fremdenhass mit neuerlicher Eindringlichkeit.
Ausgehend vom Titel die Frage, was man mit Großstädten, gar Weltstädten, assoziiert, was nicht zuletzt auf einen Begriff wie Zusammenleben eines Völkergemisches, auch von Einheimischen und Neuankömlingen bzw. Fremden (vgl. den Hinweis auf „passports“, Z. 9), hinausläuft. Ein anderer, gezielterer Einstieg ist denkbar über den Begriff „Exodus“ und seine Bedeutung (evtl. durch Schülerreferat).

Assignments

While-reading tasks

p. 37 Sketch what the different stanzas have got in common.

The poem is based on the contrast between the size and the nature of the big city that is home to millions, rich and poor alike, but has not got room enough for the refugees (l. 3). A look back at their old home, where they are no longer at home, at the church yard, where the dead have found their rest and where the life of nature is constantly renewed, underlines the fate of those whose passports are not renewed and thus not valid any more (2 and 3). The following stanzas describe their restless odyssey with their varying appeals for help: consul (4), committee (5), public meeting (6). Though the tone may change from officialese to politeness and finally to discrimination, the message is essentially the same: rejection. The indoor scene as it were turns into an outdoor scene: Nature as a sinister messenger: Hitler over Europe proclaiming death to the Jews (7). The following stanzas (8, 9, 10) present the image of the animals on earth, in the sea and in the sky who all have got their homes, because – what irony – they have got no politicians, they are no humans (10). The final two stanzas complete the frame taking up the biblical image of the house with many rooms to house everyone but with no room for them, and the final stanza referring to World War II and the extinction of the Jews.
Some striking features of the poem should be pointed out: the dialectic structure of each of the stanzas with the rhyme pairs showing the general situation and the third verse pointing out the fate of the Jews; the contrast between dehumanized civilization (!) and nature; the unemotional style (cf. the almost neutral, laconic enumeration of events like in a report; the omission of the "I" to underline the impartial role of the reporter) of the narrative and descriptive part as opposed to the highly emotional style of the third verse (cf. repetition of the assertion and the apostrophe, direct appeal) hammering the inhuman treatment of the Jews into the reader's mind.

p. 37 In an anthology of modern verse this poem is entered under "Refugee Blues." Explain.

The poem seems to have been composed in the tradition of the American Negro Spiritual, the plain rhythmic song that accompanied the work and voiced the lament of the early African-American slaves by describing their lives, their labour, their sorrows, dreams and deep-rooted hopes of redemption. The blues is a kind of secularized version of the spirituals imitating their rhythm, their sad, melancholy mood and melody and the story element and the three-line stanza. As far as protest and lamentation are concerned, it may even be compared to modern rap-songs. Taking all this into account, the editor's choice is more telling than just the index line which hints at a poem in the tradition of city lyrics.

Activities

1. Look for pictures showing big cities. Pick one that you find most adequate as an illustration to go with the poem.

City images p. 38

Of course, you can start with the picture of Chicago in the book. First describe it, then state what the picture of this city makes you think of. This task is already a preparation of Vonnegut's story (cf. task 3).
Then the students may come up with any guide book or any picture book of any city, preferably of course American cities. They should understand that their choice reflects their understanding not so much of the content but of the tone of the poem, of what they associate with this city with ten-million souls: e.g. anonymity, alienation, the people on the fringe, the sometimes overpowering and intimidating or simply inhuman architecture, the lack of human touch and spontaneity, the concrete desert, but also the charming street scenes, the picturesque atmosphere, etc.
Every student should have a suggestion and an example all of which could illustrate either the poem as a whole or individual stanzas or the controversial image of a city reflected in the poem.

2. Change the first verse of the poem into: "Say this village has two hundred souls ..." What associations come up?

p. 38

The task can be completed either as a *rewrite-exercise* or as a *creative work* trying to catch a totally different set of associations and connotations that go along with the idea of a village. Some of the ideas expressed in the poem may remain as they are, others are entirely out of place. Why?
As rewriting the whole poem demands rather a lot, rewriting just one stanza and assembling all the students' stanzas may be a sensible compromise. And why not look for pictures, paintings, sketches, photos to illustrate that new version?

3. Vonnegut's story on p. 39 occurs in Chicago, the scene from Isler's novel on p. 45 in New York. A mere coincidence?

p. 38

In addition to the first task of looking for pictures showing big cities the students might be asked to find associations linked with the cities of Chicago and New York that both received and were the first homes of millions of immigrants. Obviously, Auden, Isler and Vonnegut chose the big cities because their size and often their very names already conjure up a vivid image of the exciting and bustling, hectic and cruel, intimidating and anonymous city which, on the other hand, is home to so many and offers so much to so many. In combination with a brainstorming on the picture and on the associations with Chicago and New York the students should also read Carl Sandburg's poem "Chicago" and listen to Elvis Presley's song "In the Ghetto" which is about a boy's fate in Chicago. And why not look for poems and songs dealing with New York?

Adam Kurt Vonnegut, Jr.

Author

Kurt Vonnegut, Jr., born in 1922, a fourth-generation German-American, prominent author who in his work mingles historical, realistic elements with satire and even science fiction. Like "Adam" his novels *Slaughterhouse-Five* and *The Children's Crusade* deal with his own experiences during the bombings of Germany in the Second World War.

Synopsis of the text

The short story is about one day and one night in the life of Ava and Heinz Knechtmann, both survivors of the holocaust, who now live in Chicago. Ava has given birth to a baby-son. To Heinz after all he and Ava have been through, this is so overwhelming that he cannot understand how his fellow-Americans react. To them, life and birth are something quite normal, quite ordinary, while to Heinz it is something miraculous because he and Ava faced death and destruction.

Unterrichts-empfehlungen

Vorbemerkungen

Die Kurzgeschichte handelt von der Einzigartigkeit und Unwiederholbarkeit der Geburt eines Kindes. Darüber hinaus aber handelt die Geschichte von einem jüdischen Paar, dem gerade im Erlebnis der Geburt seines Kindes die bewusst verdrängte und folglich längst schon verloren geglaubte kulturelle Identität als deutsch-amerikanische Juden aufgeht.

Einstimmung über das Bild von Chicago als dem Ort der Handlung, aber denkbar ist auch ein Einstieg über eine Serie von Babybildern oder über eine Zusammenstellung von Geburtsanzeigen.

Assignments

While-reading-tasks

p. 39 ➤ Think about the importance of the motif of names and name-giving.

In general: Names are a part of a person's identity and calling one another by names establishes a personal contact and communication. That mythological concept (in our Western culture greatly influenced by the biblical tradition of names and name-giving) still applies to our time as well and is reflected in our fear of being reduced to statistical numbers only.

In the story the most striking observation is that most of the names in the Knechtmann family are related to the family's German past: Karl, Kroll, Heinrich, Friederich, Helga. The surname itself is a telling name which also applies to its corrupt version in the mispronounced American-English version of Netman and relates to the idea of being caught. (Note, too, the connotation of the doctor's surname: Powers, and also Heinz's co-worker's name Harry, a diminutive form like that of Heinrich/Heinz – Henry/Harry.)

Ava/Eve and Adam from Hebrew *life* and *red earth/red skin/man(kind)* stress the archetypal meaning of the story.

What is the meaning of this little phone-episode?

p. 41

The phone-booth and the phone symbolize communication. The soldier has someone, members of his family, to talk to and to share his joy while Heinz painfully realizes that he has no one to confide in (until the last scene with his wife).

What does Heinz hope to experience in the tavern; what does he really experience?

p. 42

On the surface, this is quite a normal situation: Someone wants to celebrate something and buys his friends a drink. On a deeper level, however, the situation in the tavern reveals Heinz's situation in which he has to go to a bar to meet people to share his joy, where he has to buy them a drink and has to understand that there are things like baseball that matter to them more.

Sketch how the reader s prepared for the significance of this final encounter.

p. 44

After his repeated attempts to communicate and share his joy with the people around him and after the series of more or less friendlly rebuffs, the reader, like Heinz, is prepared for the moment when Heinz meets his wife, the only one to understand the miracle of the birth of a child for someone who has been through the hell of persecution and destruction of life. It is interesting to note the reversal of roles in this final episode. It is Avchen who does most of the talking with Heinz only briefly responding. Where there is this deep understanding there is no need for many words.

Activities

1. The text can be structured according to the different reactions to the birth of his baby that Heinz encounters.

Structure and symbolism p. 44

(1) Waiting for the baby, (2) Heinz and his past in Nazi-Germany, (3) the announcement of the birth and Heinz's immediate reaction: gratitude, (4) professional detachment of the doctor and the nurses, (5) contrasting episode: community of shared joy opposed to Heinz's loneliness, (6) tavern episode: the co-drinkers' baby-boom routine opposed to the unique significance of the birth of a baby, (7) Harry's conventional reaction as an expression of his inability to understand the miracle, (8) Heinz's growing awareness of his isolation, his criticism of American society with its lack of concern and his retreat to his long forgotten sources, (9) next morning return to the hospital: communication with Avchen, community based on love and the common fate of persecution of the Jews which makes you re-evaluate life.

2. Names are important with regard to a person's identity. How is this topic treated in the story?

Heinz is extremely conscious of names, constantly reflects on his relatives' names because they symbolize continuation after death and extinction – contrary to the Americans, who, like the soldier, either don't know about a name or mispronounce it, abbreviate or reduce it to initials.

The use of stereotypes ➤
p. 44

1. To some extent, Vonnegut makes use of certain national and cultural stereotypes (cf. Heinz's reaction to life in this big American city). What is the function of these stereotypes in the story?

Jews: nose; intellectual attitude; important scientists, doctors, artists; obsession with the past, history and memory; Nazi terror, concentration camp, displaced persons.
Americans: Chicago, big city, loud, hectic; professional attitude; concentration on baseball; ignorant but friendly; superficial.
Stereotypes are used here to make the difference visible between people who take life as something normal and unspectacular and those to whom it is a wonder because they have been through hell.

2. From the information the text gives you, write a brief characterization of Heinz and one of the other characters.

Heinz, 22, but looks older, "ugly … almost to be beautiful" (because of some innate qualities); a presser with great dreams and great memories of the past, married to Ava, his soul's companion; young man trying to integrate into the new society and to share his joy with people; un-American in many ways: introverted, extremely serious and thought-tormented; lives a secluded life, does not share enthusiasm for baseball, etc.
Sousa (use of surname to stress the distance, cf. mentioning profession), athletic figure, outgoing and outspoken, rather rude; father of seven girls now, male patriarch, sexist attitude; domineering; insensitive to emotions of others; superficially friendly, baseball fan.

Situation and role ➤
p. 45

1. Prepare a role-card for one of the characters to prepare him or her for an encounter with Heinz. Remember: What kind of person is he or she? What is the situation like? What does he or she say in the dialogue, how do they interact with Heinz?

Character: Heinz and Sousa, see above and underline what you think most important for your acting; internalize the information, slip into Heinz's shoes; **situation**: e.g. the two in front of the glass panel looking at their new-born children; **dialogue**: S: I had hoped so much this time it would be a boy, my son … H: I couldn't care less …

2. Imagine that Heinz Knechtmann has finally decided to visit Germany after many, many years, and you and your class talk to him about the Germany of today.

Ask one of the students to play Heinz's part. All the others prepare questions to be put to him. The interview can be a hot seat exercise. You can start like this: What made you finally come back? … You said you never wanted to use German again. Why? … Has your attitude changed …?

We Were Germans Alan Isler

Author

Alan Isler was born in London in 1934, went to the United States to teach English Literature at the University of New York and returned to London in 1995. The novel was his first novel.

Synopsis of the text

Otto Kroner, the first-person narrator, inhabitant of the Emma Lazarus, describes his way into exile and the meaning of things of the past and then recalls the events of 3 April, 1933. Three generations of the Körner family of Nuremberg experience the outbreak of Nazi-terror against the Jews. Their reactions greatly differ between utter disbelief, indifference, fear and (vain) hope. Otto himself completely misinterprets the signs on the wall and talks his family into staying instead of emigrating in time in order to be saved. His untimely hesitation costs the lives of his family, including that of his son Hugo.

Unterrichtsempfehlungen

Vorbemerkungen
Erinnerung und Schuld prägen diese Szene, die sehr eindringlich und anschaulich belegt, wie Juden die Bedrohung durch die Nazis unterschätzten. Erst im Rückblick lässt sich das Undenkbare denken; damit wird zugleich auch die eigene Schuld deutlich. Zur Vertiefung ein Zitat von David Daiches: *"Jewish unity is a matter of memory, conscious or unconscious. When the memory goes, the unity will go."* Ein Einstieg kann dadurch erfolgen, dass man statt *unity* den Begriff *identity* einsetzt und mit einem Rückblick auf Momente des eigenen Lebens verknüpft. Mit der Betrachtung der Bildcollage schlägt man den Bogen zurück zu Isler.

Assignments

Pre-reading task

Before you read, look back on important moments in your life.

The living past p. 45

As a homework task, prepare notes on an important moment in your life. Then present your episode. Vividly describe what happened, then explain why you remember it and finally sketch its significance in your life.

While-readings tasks

The home bears the name of Emma Lazarus. Why?

p. 46

Emma Lazarus, born in New York in 1849, died in 1887, was the poet who wrote "The New Colossus", a poem on America's role as a haven for the persecuted, the "tired" and the "poor" of the world. Her poem is inscribed on the base of the Statue of Liberty.

p. 46 ➤

Think of what makes people "pack up" their memories. What makes them take them out again?

Subconscious suppression above all of sad memories, of violent deaths, "snapshots of family misery"; you just don't wish to think about it hoping that barring it from your memory you spare yourself the negative effects. In critical moments, however, you retreat to your memories as part of your life story, your identity. You are looking for the pattern behind it all, asking what made you what you are.

p. 46 ➤

What makes the son so important to the narrator (cf. Vonnegut's *Adam*)?

The fact that he had a son, that his only son is dead now and that his family will be extinct, that there will be no continuation after he is gone – and that it is all, at least partly, his own guilt. Vonnegut's "Adam": The first son, Karl, died, but with the birth of Peter Karl life has begun again; the family tradition is continued, life (cf. Avchen – hava=life) has triumphed over death.

p. 46 ➤

How does the narrator make the reader feel that this day is so extraordinary?

By giving the exact historical date first, not as an act of the narrator's decision but as an act of major force. The reader knows what happened and can thus judge action and reaction of the characters and is aware of the tragic outcome of Otto's naive reasoning.

p. 47 ➤

What made Otto's obvious misunderstanding so fatal and tragic?

Death that he could have foreseen; his insight comes too late. His arrogance cost the lives of his family.

Activities

1933: a year that changed Germany p. 48 ➤

1. Check in a history book or on CD-ROM what you can find on the events in 1933. Make a list of the important events

You can use e.g. TIME-Almanach on CD-ROM, *Encarta* but also *Page One* which gives you a collection of the decisive articles of the New York Herald Tribune. Pick out keywords, central events, personalities, political activities, national and international politics, etc.

2. Add the information the text provides. Explain what Isler's account adds to the historical facts.

View from without and view from within – history on the level of a "domestic scene"; the human factor: history written in terms of human fates; how Nazi-ideology and Nazi-politics affected Jewish families who thought they were Germans and were proud of it; the tragic sense of being too late; and the irony, if only the intellectually superior and sober members of the family had listened to the emotions and hysterics of a woman; the enormous guilt that Otto Kroner has carried all his life, that he was responsible for the death of his family.

Maus. A Survivor's Tale

Art Spiegelman

Author

Prominent American cartoonist of Polish-Jewish descent who with his *Maus* boldly created the historical and biographical picture book in the comic-strip tradition, at the same time reviving the tradition of the moral tales for children.

Synopsis of the text

Artie (autobiographical cartoonist/narrator) reflects on his project of presenting the history of Auschwitz, the holocaust and the loss of his brother in a comic. The story of the loss of his brother is drawn and narrated by a grown-up taking the point of view of a child which results in insight of the adult plus innocent directness of the child; the naivety and the simplicity of a child make the monstrosity of the holocaust all the more moving.

Assignments

While-reading activities

Auschwitz, the holocaust – in a comic?

◄ p. 48

A fundamental question. Against the background of what we (or more precisely: Americans) normally find in comics this is something new. With regard to the dignity and seriousness of the topic and the emotional response of the Jewish survivors it is on the verge of sacrilege. New trends of combining information, instruction and teaching with entertainment, of using the popular medium and the popularity of comic strips among all the nation(s) have contributed to the acceptance and the success of Spiegelman's tale and have helped to keep the memory of the holocaust and its victims alive (cf. Walter Moers: *Adolf, die Nazi-Sau.* Frankfurt: Eichborn 1998).

Maus. A Survivor's Tale – for young and old?

◄ p. 48

At face value: for young readers. The cartoonist tells the story of his parents' life in Poland under Nazi-occupation looking back on his life after they all escaped to the States. The loss of his brother and his parents' unsuccessful efforts to trace him lead to Artie's rivalry with his ideal of a brother. This and the nightmare of a perfect killing-machinery and finally his desire to have known for himself what his parents had to go through, most certainly appeals to children. The weighing of the question of how appropriate this form of art is for that specific topic and, above all, whether any art can reconstruct a reality "worse than (his) darkest dreams" aims at the aesthetic-minded and discerning reader, as a rule: an adult. Moreover, the black and white, highly stylized (almost "primitive") drawing technique that concentrates on the elementary and only hints at the emotional aura is meant to stimulate the reader's participation as to how to picture and verbalize what is actually beyond imagination in images and words.

p. 48

Characterize the role of the brother.

More than just his biological brother; personification of brotherhood, but also symbolizing our relationship to the dear ones that we have lost and that are consequently idealized (perhaps as a compensation for the life they had to give up so soon).

p. 49

What does the dialogue tell you about the importance of the past?

The topic of the dialogue is past and memory, the fact that one cannot escape what has shaped the fate of one's family. One way of preserving the past and our memory is to write it down in the form that is most appropriate to you, i. e. the cartoonist Art Spiegelman who writes down what his father tells him about his family's exodus.

Activities

No limits to comics? p. 50

1. Show in what way this scene from the comic-strip varies the theme of guilt.

For comparison it is advisable to consult Alan Isler's presentation of this theme.
Here, the complex historical guilt is presented in the form of a very personal evaluation of not feeling guilty about his rivalry with his dead brother (question of a kind of universal guilt: Why him, not me?) but of feeling guilty of having been spared what his parents had to go through. Knowing about their suffering and his own having had "an easier life than they did" are sensations based on compassion, not on moral failure.

2. Think of a possible continuation of the dialogue trying "to do it as a comic strip" in the manner of Spiegelman's tale.

Starting point: "Maybe I ought to forget about the whole thing." What can be said for or against continuing writing and drawing cartoons about Auschwitz and the holocaust? Some possible arguments or positions. "Better concentrate on today – forget about the past …" "But, can't you see, he was my brother … and who would remember later, if …".

3. Could you imagine a German comic strip on e.g. Auschwitz?

Younger people may take a different view, and there are some who just don't bother, but most Germans, especially of the older generation, would probably say no to the question, for two reasons: There is a shyness to touch on that precarious question of the guilt of the agents responsible for the six million Jewish victims of Nazi-terror; and there is a lack of detachment necessary to do justice even to those who did not speak up to or act against the atrocities. A third reason may be the highly critical, perhaps even hypercritical attitude of the international public tired of the excuses and the unwillingness to accept responsibility but also too biased to make distinctions between *the* Germans.

4. Now read the following excerpt from a review on such a satirical comic strip in the American press. Comment on the difference between Spiegelman's and Moers' work.

The headline of the review refers to the obvious incompatibility of Hitler's role in European politics and world history and a humorous treatment in the comic strip tradition, though there can be no doubt about the satirical intention of the book (cf. title, the "portrait" of Hitler, and the dialect statement of Hitler in the bubble). The reviewer, first of all, contrasts the satire, by definition critical of political leaders and the attitudes of the powerful, with a potential reaction of "Der Führer" (sic!) (annoyance) and the controversial response to the work among German readers (laughter, eyebrows, hackles). The seriousness of the adult comic and the debate it has triggered are underlined not only by the number of copies sold but even more by the reaction of serious publications, among them the FAZ, which compared Moers to Spiegelman. The artistic quality of the drawing, the language register used and the level of argumentation, however, seem to indicate a less serious treatment of the topic compared with Spiegelman's *Maus*.

Chapter 4: Fears and Hopes – Mind-Shaping and Habit-Forming

Vorbemerkungen zum Kapitel

Nachdem die ersten beiden Kapitel Probleme der so genannten *hyphenated Americans* und das dritte Kapitel die besondere Problematik der *Jewish-Americans* und ihrer Bindung an Deutschland thematisiert haben, lenkt das letzte Kapitel den Blick auf das Bild des Deutschen, sein eigenes wie das, das sich Andere von ihm machen. Ganz bewusst sind hier Beispiele aus der weit verbreiteten neueren Reiseliteratur gewählt worden, weil sie schon allein durch ihre Popularität eine viel weiter reichende Breitenwirkung hat als zwar feingeistige, aber doch auf einen sehr elitären Leserkreis beschränkte sozialpolitische, geistesgeschichtliche oder literatursoziologische Publikationen, die im Rahmen eines Leistungskurses jedoch unbedingt zur Vertiefung herangezogen werden sollten (Günter Trautmann (Hg.): *Die hässlichen Deutschen?* Deutschland im Spiegel der westlichen und östlichen Nachbarn, Darmstadt, Wissenschaftliche Buchgesellschaft, 1991; Ansgar und Vera Nünning: *Der Deutsche an sich*. Einem Phantom auf der Spur, München, dtv, 1994; Günther Blaicher: *Das Deutschlandbild in der englischen Literatur*, Darmstadt, Wissenschaftliche Buchgesellschaft, 1992; Harald Husemann (Hg.): *As Others See Us*. The Presentation of Germany and the Germans in England, Paderborn, Schöningh, 1984). Beispiele von Trainingsprogrammen für in Europa tätige US-amerikanische Manager und Frauen im internationalen Geschäftsleben, die auf der vergleichenden Kulturpsychologie aufbauen, und eine Einführung in den Zusammenhang zwischen Kulturstandards und Geschichtserfahrung wollen zum Nachvollzug und zur kritischen Revision und Relativierung der eigenen Urteile und Vorurteile anregen.

Start here

Why communication often fails p. 51

Think of factors that can influence communication and interaction either positively or negatively.

Ausgangspunkt eines *brainstorming* sollte das Gemälde des in den Staaten sehr populären Malers und Zeitschriften-Illustrators sein, der das Zusammenleben von Menschen verschiedener Hautfarbe, Nationen, Ethnien und Kulturen – nicht zuletzt vielleicht unter religiösen Gesichtspunkten, vgl. das Bibelzitat – idealisiert. Es ist zu erwarten, dass die Schülerinnen und Schüler Rockwells Sicht mit einer realistischeren Beschreibung von Problemen und Konflikten in täglicher Kommunikation und Interaktion, von Partnerschaft und Familie bis zum Zusammenleben der Völker, kontrastieren werden.

Positive factors: love, friendship, sympathy, solidarity, understanding, tolerance, alliances, necessity of cooperation, common goals or interests, etc.; **negative factors**: hatred, dislike, animosity, envy, jealousy, misunderstanding and intolerance, competition and rivalry, different or opposing goals and interests, arrogance, fight for power, status, and prestige, etc.

Then consult the "iceberg-model" below. What does it try to show? Would you organize the factors in the same way?

Below the surface of objectivity and neutral, unbiased, impartial behaviour there are many claims, concerns and hidden feelings of *angst* which the partners communicating, negotiating and interacting are not even aware of. However, they influence their attitudes and actions: The deeper they lie, the more difficult they are to overcome, the less predictable and thus calculable are attitudes and actions based on them.
Other ways of grouping depend on a personal interpretation of the importance of these factors in one's own way of interacting with people (e. g. dominance of positive or negative factors).

Present the model in English; translate the terminology first.

Terminology: objectivity, business-mindedness (matter-of-factness), conflicting goals, power, influence, coalitions, alliances, prestige, competition (rivalry), recognition, dependence, hurt feelings, disappointment, angst, sympathy, animosity, antipathy;
Presentation of the model by applying it to a case, such as examples from school: destination and itinerary of the Grand Study Tour in the 12th or 13th grade, etc.

The Germans – How They See Others and Themselves

Stefan Zeidenitz and Ben Barkow

Authors

Both authors are Germans now living in Britain and overseas and teaching German there. In their careers they also taught English in Germany.

Synopsis of the text

First, how the Germans see the English (love, adore, role model), the Americans (respect, affection, headmaster), the Italians (common history, similar nationhood: attraction, friendship, appreciation), the French (admiration of their civilization, pity with their inferior culture, Francophilia), the Mediterranean people (envy of relaxed life-style, culture and climate), the Swiss (unrivalled in Teutonic virtues, e. g. order, punctuality, diligence, cleanliness, thoroughness). **Second**, how the Germans see themselves: looking for harmony, tolerant, sociable, modest, ordinary (beer, *Wurst*, *Gemütlichkeit*), simple, honest folk; romantic, prone to speculation, complicated philosophy; know everything better.

Unterrichts-empfehlungen

Vorbemerkungen
Die drei folgenden Beiträge sollten u. a. unter dem Aspekt besprochen werden, wie der jeweilige Standpunkt der Autoren (*point of view 1/2/3*) ihre Sicht der Deutschen und ihre Interpretation des Verhältnisses der Deutschen zu ihren Nachbarn bedingt oder doch zumindest beeinflusst.
Möglichkeit der Bearbeitung der Texte in arbeitsteiliger Gruppenarbeit: Präsentieren der Ergebnisse im Plenum als Schrittfolge von Informieren, Kommentieren, Argumentieren.

Assignments

Pre-reading task

The importance of the point of view (1) p. 52

Both authors, teachers and freelance writers, were born in Germany and left it for England. They taught German and promoted German culture in England and Japan and English culture in Germany. What does the information add to your expectation?

Balanced view, preference for the English, more global perspective, critical comparisons; tendency to view the Germans more critically (as members of the family so to speak), etc.

Activities

Promoting understanding p. 53

1. The title of this series of travel guides is *Xenophobe's guide to …*, here: *the Germans*. If you were the series editor, what title would you choose for your guides?

Suggestions: Traveller's, Visitor's, Globetrotter's, Cosmopolitan's Guide or Insiders view of… or Meet the Germans, What you always wanted to know about the Germans, etc.

2. On the back of the book you find the definition of *xenophobia* – "an irrational fear of foreigners, probably justified, always understandable." A good example of sales promotion? Give your definition to attract readers.

Use of a trendy catchword, provocative, slightly ironical, aimed at the critical intellectual individualist; a definition to attract other readers (who do not wish to be politically correct); Xenophobia – a fear of foreigners often based on the lack of personal, first-hand experience. So why not find out about Germany and the Germans for yourself – now!

3. Analyze the illustration on the cover. What is it meant to stimulate? Think of an alternative and sketch it.

Visualization of beer, *Wurst* (mentioned in the preface) and of nationalism and military past (or present?) as a sort of confirmation of prejudices that are widely held. An alternative cover might put together other motifs that among others appeal to young travellers and travellers with a wide range of interests: natural beauty of the countryside, famous sights, portraits of Goethe or Beethoven, Steffi Graf or Boris Becker, famous brands, makes of car, etc.

German Characteristics

Richard Lord

Author

The author is a journalist who came to Germany, met a girl here who made him stay.

Synopsis of the text

Lines on mankind lost in darkness, "never ... happy or good" can serve to describe Germany and the Germans after the Second World War. The German paradox: In spite of all the achievements "a sense of insecurity." German history as the answer to the German character, especially the Nazi experience. Its influences can be seen in the Germans' distrust of authority, less respect for uniforms and scepticism of the military. Another effect: Many Germans are judged by the Nazi experience because critics regard the German Third Reich as an unparalleled crime that cannot be washed away and thus makes Germans hide their national or cultural identity.

Unterrichts-empfehlungen

Vorbemerkungen
Subjektivere (vgl. Biografie) und doch zugleich fundiertere, ernsthaftere Deutung des Charakters des Deutschen aus seiner (jüngsten) Geschichte. Thematisierung des *point of view (2)*: Vom Außenstehenden zum Insider werden; *mixed marriage* als Akkulturation.

Assignments

Pre-reading task

The author has dedicated his book to "Gudrun, the main reason that I've stayed in Germany." What does such a rather personal remark tell you about the writer's attitude towards the country he wishes to introduce to the reader?

The importance of the point of view (2) p. 53

What, on the face of things, may be viewed as a handicap, a lack of objectivity, is the advantage of the book which can obviously claim that it was written with sympathy and an insight based on intimate knowledge of everyday life and the ordinary people.

While-reading task

Interpret Joyce's, the Irishman's, metaphor of the (mega-)nightmare.

p. 54

James Joyce's whole œuvre can be considered as the artist's effort to deal with his personal, cultural and national identity, and consequently with his past. History is viewed as the collective past that normally you as an individual have neither caused, have not been a part of and cannot be – with reason – held responsible for. In the case of the Germans' traumatic Nazi-experience, dealing with the past is indeed a nightmare: Germans, though they cannot be regarded as collectively guilty (*Kollektivschuld*), feel something like a collective shame (*Kollektivscham*, a term coined by the first German post-war President Theodor Heuss).

Activities

What kind of traveller is addressed? p. 55

1. This series is called *Culture Shock!* List some of the connotations.

Being exposed to a culture that is so different, behind or ahead of one's own cultural environment that it causes an unpleasant, loathsome, precarious, threatening and dangerous reaction.

2. The preceding text was written by two Germans looking back on Germany from outside. This text was written by an Englishman living in Germany. Try to trace the difference.

Speaking as insiders from without, as an outsider from within; variation of auto- and hetero-stereotypes; detachment as a role or an attitude taken on and resulting in irony, sometimes even sarcasm or cynisism vs. involvement and compassion as a mental habit, intellectual wittiness vs. emotional intelligence; judgement vs. participation, etc.

3. Friends from England plan a trip to Germany. Which of the two travel guides would you personally recommend? Write them a note.

Based on the qualifications of the authors and their particular relationship to Germany and the Germans (see under 2) make a decision using some of the arguments given above.

4. On the front and the back cover of the book you find the following illustrations. How do you think a potential buyer reacts to them? Compare this cover to that of *Xenophobia.*

The sales strategy of the *Xenophobe's* guide seems to aim at a confirmation of prejudices as a kind of sophisticated entertainment while *Culture Shock!* seems to aim at understanding Germans and their "customs and etiquette" and what helped to shape them; warning to believe in "positively harmful" clichés.

Manners and Mannerisms – The English and the Germans

George Mikes

Author

Born in Hungary in 1912 where he went to university and was awarded a doctorate in law. He went to England as a journalist and stayed there. He has written many humorous books on the characters of different nations, e.g. the English, the Americans, the Germans, etc.

Synopsis of the text

This satirical sketch is about understatement, a character trait often attributed to the English. It means that you pretend to be or know less than you really do. A German, unaware of this convention, spoils the situation.

Unterrichtsempfehlungen

Vorbemerkungen

1. Schwerpunkt
Der Zusammenhang zwischen *manners* (*mannerisms*), *norms, conventions, rules and culture standards* als Ergebnis sprachgemeinschaftlich bedingter Kulturerfahrung.

2. Schwerpunkt
Die zweischneidige Kritik der Satire an sinnentleerten Konventionen (*not knowing anything*) und verkrusteten Verhaltensformen (*prejudice; knowing everything better*); Erzählstandpunkt (vgl. Biografie des Autors als Mann zwischen den Welten) über der Situation, relativierend und ironisierend.

Assignments

While-reading task

p. 56

Understanding humour – a test of tolerance?

A tricky question. According to popular belief, having a good sense of humour means that one is able to laugh about oneself and one's own follies. One should not take oneself too seriously. Popular media, especially the tabloid press, all over the world know that appealing to prejudices helps to sell. Sometimes, however, they go too far. Remember, this does not mean that *the English*, etc. don't like the Germans.

Activities

National character and humour p. 57

1. Study the little sketch by Mikes closely. Point out the humorous elements.

Contrary to the general truth that knowledge is power, Mikes presents a set of absurd rules ("must never really learn anything"), pseudo-logically supported by an even more absurd argument taken from basic algebra; clear decisions (yes or no) denounced as rude. The apparent shortcomings of the dinner guests directly contradict their background and expertise and would make them look ridiculous if it was not for the demonstration of the two English national character traits or social conventions: understatement and small talk. English understatement hiding competence is opposed to German unasked for display of "competence and achievement" (Lord, p. 54) and of "know(ing) everything better" (Zeidenitz / Barkow, p. 53). Witty characterization of the members of the English upper-middle class, precise presentation of their behaviour, including their linguistic behaviour; speaking and conversing as a social ritual, as "art"; climactic structure of the episode resulting in a play on words and prejudices or stereotypes: The *colonel* raises associations of the military past, the *bishop* in his reaction turns the Christian commandment of love into its opposite.

2. Divide the different roles among the members of your class, and act out the dialogue trying to catch the sense of humour.

Preparation and presentation of the text as a dramatic sketch (cf Freddy Frinton in *Dinner for One. The Ninetieth Birthday*).

3. Explain what this satire makes fun of and thus criticizes. Is it only about the Germans?

Only marginal criticism of the Germans; the criticism of a society that puts meaningless social conventions such as ritualized understatement and small talk for small talk's sake above all is more important: criticizing by ridiculing.

Stereotyping in cartoons **p. 57**

1. Look at the cartoons. Explain how British cartoonists see the Germans.

Essentially as domineering, arrogant, Prussian-type holiday-goers claiming their deckchairs, wanting to be loved by the British; as a nation whose national character was closely scrutinized by an expert commission set up by Mrs Thatcher, then Prime Minister, with the results put together for a board-meeting; finally, as the caricature of the fat and ostentatiously rich, Bavarian-type German (ironically with the sign of victory that Winston Churchill popularized to cheer up his fellow-citizens in the war against Germany) wearing an I-love-you-button.

2. Find examples in German newspapers and magazines illustrating how German cartoonists see the Germans, the British or other nations.

Work in groups or with a partner. Prepare newspaper-clippings. Group them according to criteria such as (1) nationalities presented, (2) hetero- or autostereotypes, (3) national character traits criticized, (4) publication in the quality or the popular press, (5) development of the image of the German/English/American … in comparison with earlier cartoons, e.g. of the sixties, seventies …

3. Make a collage of these cartoons to be displayed in the classroom. Prepare a contribution on "How We See Each Other" for an exhibition on Intercultural Relations.

Possible individual tasks:
(1) Write a short introduction to a catalogue of the exhibition. (2) Prepare a guided tour through the exhibition picking out and commenting on the highlights. (3) Write and print out in a professional way short comments on the cartoons as sort of guidelines to go with their presentation in the showcases.(4) Assemble your own collection in your portfolio, and explain it in a short comment.

History and Culture Standards

Karl Markowsky and Alexander Thomas

Authors

Both authors are psychologists at the University of Regensburg. Their special field is culture psychology, a comparative study of how the common experience of a speech community shapes their members' culture standards and consequently their behaviour and interaction with members of other nations or ethnic groups. They are the authors of training programmes for Germans going to the United States and to Britain and for Americans coming to Germany.

Synopsis of the text

Situation: The question of whether to use "Sie" or "du" arises for American students staying in a German family. Four answers are given to explain why the host father asked them if he could use "du".
Explanations throw light on the culture standards behind the different behaviour as expressed in the answers.
The historical background explains the genesis of the underlying culture standard of "interpersonal differentiation" (*interpersonale Distanzregulierung*), which should by no means be misinterpreted as lack of sympathy.

Unterrichtsempfehlungen

Vorbemerkungen
Dieser Auszug aus dem kulturpsychologischen Vergleich zwischen dem Verhalten von Amerikanern und Deutschen dient einmal dazu, die vorangegangenen Beobachtungen theoretisch zu untermauern. Andererseits soll der Wechselbezug zwischen der Beobachtung von alltäglichen kritischen Interaktionen, dem eigenen Deutungsversuch und der systematisierenden kulturpsychologischen Erklärung der Phänomene aufgehellt werden, um selbstständig mit den folgenden Beispielen aus interkulturellen Trainingsprogrammen arbeiten zu können.
Die Auseinandersetzung mit der von Markowsky und Thomas gewählten Situation und ihrer Problematisierung, die Deutung der möglichen Einzelantworten und der Versuch ihrer Generalisierung sollten in zwei Schritten erfolgen:
(1) Analyse der **Situation** in Einzelarbeit, Entscheidung für eine der Auswahlantworten und deren Diskussion in Partnerarbeit; erst im Anschluss daran Lektüre der ***Explanations*** und Zusammenfasung der Argumente und wertende Stellungnahme (Zustimmung, Ablehnung, Modifikation).
(2) Analyse von ***The historical background*** unter dem Aspekt, was eigentlich *typically German* an dieser Geschichtserfahrung ist (z.B. *permanent state of isolation from the outside world*, etc.); allerdings auch die Möglichkeit, anders als das Englische es kann, auf psychische und soziale Befindlichkeit mit sprachlichen Formen differenziert zu reagieren (*du, Sie* vs. *you*).

Assignments

Pre-reading task

Critical interaction p. 58

Before you study the following example of a critical interaction think about attitudes and forms of behaviour that you think are typically German or at least apply to many Germans. ...
Can you think of more German culture standards?

You should check the preceding texts again and name some of the typically German qualities or behaviours.
Here are some American culture standards for comparison: Patriotism, Egalitarianism, Easy Going, Activity-Centeredness, Competitiveness, Individualism, Social Acceptance, etc.

Activities

Applying and modifying the theory p. 61

1. The culture standard underlying the above situation is called "interpersonal differentiation". Give your own definition of the term.

In addition to what Markowsky and Thomas have found out you may argue that the US have had a much longer democratic tradition, with less regard for authorities (whatever their nature: age, class, origin, position, status, education, etc.). Moreover, Americans tend to be more flexible, which also shows in their easygoing and casual behaviour as opposed to a more formal behaviour of the Germans; note also the linguistic differentiation (*Sie, du, you*).

2. Among other German culture standards the authors name the following: rule-orientation, respect for authority, the need to organize, personal property or compulsory sense of duty. Imagine situations demonstrating these culture standards. Where would punctuality belong?

Conventions, rules, norms regulate and organize living together, especially where there is much less space than in a country like the US. On the whole, Germans are not only quite willing to accept certain rules, forms of polite and more formal behaviour and dress-code but tend to ask for rules where there are none (so far). **Respect for authority**: Think of the hierarchy in a German firm or in the German administration or the function of titles. **The need to organize**: Think of your school community, your class, your spare time, your leisure activities with all their organizational needs which limit your individual freedom. What is typically German about them, and where do you think you could and would like to do with less? **Personal property**: Visit a German home or an office. You always find the doors closed while in the US there is an "open-door-policy". Why? **Compulsory sense of duty**: It is not an innate quality of the Germans but a result of many interdependent factors such as those mentioned before. Due to them the acceptance of one's duty is still a high value, the disobedience of which is sanctioned even in the smallest community like the family. **Punctuality** relates to rule orientation.

3. Patriotism is a central culture standard of the Americans. There is no such standard for the Germans. What reasons can you think of?

The wars, especially World War II, the Third Reich with its atrocities, the holocaust, a divided country up to ten years ago, a separate identity and loyalty of the Germans living in the Eastern and the Western parts, a general distrust of national symbols and emblems (cf. flags) and patriotic institutions or ceremonies.

4. Everyone who has ever been abroad remembers an incident that she or he found strange, funny or even irritating. Describe one or more and find an explanation applying culture standards as presented above.

Consider this example for a start: It is from the popular humorous writer Erma Bombeck's collection of travel anecdotes (*When You Look Like Your Passport Photo, It's Time to Go Home,* pp. 170–171):

"I live in Arizona where tourism is big business. One night at one of our popular cowboy steak houses, I watched a group of visiting Japanese men. They had watched a shoot-out, visited a saloon, and allowed themselves to be photographed wearing cowboy hats and six-shooters over their hips.When they sat down to dinner, one of them must have ordered his steak well-done, because he was served a dusty boot on a plate. Just as their steak knives were poised over their meat, a waitress came by with a pair of scissors and cut all their neckties in half. They just sat there – not speaking – as she stapled half of their ties to the ceiling with their calling cards.
They had to wonder how we won the war."

Can you explain the meaning of this anecdote? Then, think of some yourselves.

5. Sketch a situation based on your experience. Work out a dialogue with your partner and act it in class.

At least one or two examples should be given by the students. Here is an example to help them find some of their own: You had lunch in an American restaurant and haven't thought of leaving a tip of 10–15% of the bill for the waitress. You are just on your way out when she stops you …

6. Theory is not reality but a construction or an interpretation of it. There are factors that quite obviously limit the theory. Explain how e.g. age, gender, social background, education or religious belief might influence your culture standards and consequently your behaviour.

The training programmes were originally written for students and interns and were based on material supplied by them. Show how age or gender make a difference in the following examples: An American couple, your parents' friends, has invited you to spend a Sunday with them. You would like to bring your girl-friend. … Or: Your Mormon host family has invited you to join them for their Sunday service. You are Catholic/Protestant. … Or: A group of male American students (all over 21) has invited you to join them for a baseball game and for a beer afterwards. Explain to your host family how you as an 18-year-old German girl are going to handle the invitation. …

7. The American artist Duane Hanson (1926–1996) created near-to-life sculptures representing Americans – only Americans? State what makes the couple below so typical.

Both are heavy-weight (politically correct usage: persons of size), casually dressed (comfort before elegance or fashion), comfortable footwear, bold combination of colours and designs (question of taste and life-style), baseball cap, sunshade, shopping bags, camera-equipment – in the pose of the (to Hanson: American) tourist on a sight-seeing tour and shopping spree … A French woman visiting the Duane-Hanson-Exhibition in Cologne mistook the couple for German tourists. An explanation could concentrate on something all tourists have in common no matter where they are from (casual wear, cameras, shopping bags; attitude of the sightseer, etc.); but there is something that is less stylish, less elegant, less mundane that the French lady probably thought was German in comparison to the French. This is where a notion like class may come in.

Testing Your Culture-Gender Awareness

Roger E. Axtell, Tami Briggs, Margaret Corcoran, Beth Lamb

Authors

The authors were or are working in various functions (as Vice-President of one of the best-known brand names on the international market, as Principal or as consultants and trainers) in American businesses and cross-cultural business training centres.

Synopsis of the text

Three representative situations American business women encounter all over the world (here: Latin America, Middle East, Europe which because of many similarities is compared to the US) are described. In all three cases the women have to overcome certain problems related to their gender. The answers in the quiz reveal a different degree of intercultural competence and personal risk-taking.

Unterrichts-empfehlungen

Vorbemerkungen

Das Culture-Gender Awareness Quiz ist der Tabelle zum interkulturellen Trainingsprogramm vorgeschaltet. Es zielt sowohl auf eine erste Selbsteinschätzung als auch auf Motivation des (weiblichen) Benutzers ab und schärft das Gespür für die besondere Problematik der Frau im internationalen Geschäftsleben.
Der Einstieg sollte über den Hinweis auf die veränderte Rolle der Frau im internationalen Geschäftsleben erfolgen. Die wirtschaftli-

chen und finanziellen Konsequenzen, die interkulturelles „Fehlverhalten“ zur Folge haben kann, sollten erarbeitet werden; wichtig ist aber auch, dass die psychischen und sozialen Kosequenzen für die betroffenen Frauen (*success or failure, continuous effort or retreat*) deutlich angesprochen werden.
Das Quiz sollte, wie in der Einführung zum Text im Schülerbuch dargestellt, durchgeführt werden.

European and American Cultural Behaviours: How We Perceive Each Other

Authors

A team of consultants working for the American automobile industry. The joint operations of American and German car-builders has made a better understanding of each other a crucial issue.

Synopsis of the text

The table juxtaposes 16 different American and European cultural behaviours and explains how the Americans and the Europeans see their own behaviour and that of the other one. It turns out that American and European behaviours are often diametrically opposed (e.g.trust more/trust less) and sometimes reveal an antagonism (e.g. socially irresponsible/blind obedience) that, because of the effects of globalization, is no longer absolutely true.

Unterrichtsempfehlungen

Vorbemerkungen
Mit dieser Tabelle arbeitet z.B. die internationale Hauptverwaltung von Ford in Dearborn, Michigan, um ihre Mitarbeiter auf interkulturelle Unterschiede und mögliche kritische Interaktion mit europäischen Geschäftspartnern und Mitarbeitern vorzubereiten.
Zunächst empfiehlt sich die Lektüre der Tabelle in häuslicher Vorbereitung.

1. Schwerpunkt
In der Hausaufgabe wählen die Schülerinnen und Schüler die Verhaltensweisen, die ihnen besonders wichtig, richtig, sympathisch oder einfach auch falsch oder wenig repräsentativ erscheinen, und begründen ihre Entscheidung. Hier sollten, die Unterschiedlichkeit der Schülerbeiträge aufgreifend, auch die subjektive Wahrnehmung und die darauf gegründete Urteilsbildung angesprochen werden.

2. Schwerpunkt
Erörterung der zwangsläufigen Verallgemeinerung historisch gewachsener nationaler Unterschiede zunächst generell, was den Forschungsansatz angeht (*die* Amerikaner/*die* Europäer), dann die Nivellierung speziell der historisch gewachsenen nationalen Unterschiede bei den Europäern durch die Gegenüberstellung von

US-Americans and Europeans. Hier ist ein Hinweis auf das *Being and Becoming American* mit seinen das Gefühl und Bewusstsein nationaler Identität stiftenden Werten und *concepts of the mind* ganz entscheidend (vgl. dazu William W. Cutler, III: "On Being and Becoming an American", in PRAXIS 2/1992, S. 203–206). Der Unterschied zu Europa mit seinen so vielfältigen und unterschiedlichen Bausteinen nationaler und kultureller (man denke nur an die Sprachenvielfalt!) Identität liegt auf der Hand und dürfte auch selbst durch die zukünftigen Vereinigten Staaten von Europa nur geringfügig abgeschliffen und eingeebnet werden. Die Tabelle sollte aber auch dafür sensibilisieren, dass Amerikaner und Europäer und die europäischen Nachbarn untereinander vieles gemeinsam haben, das man nicht zuletzt dann begreift, wenn man in Offenheit und aktiver Wertschätzung über die Unterschiede nachgedacht hat.

Teil III

Klausurbeispiele

Klausur 1

A Modern Tale of Racial Discord

John Grisham

From the opening passage of the novel *The Chamber*, published in 1994.

The decision to bomb the office of the radical Jew lawyer was reached with relative ease. Only three people were involved in the process. The first was the man with the money. The second was a local operative who knew the territory. And the third was a young patriot and zealot with a talent for explosives and an astonishing knack for disappearing without a trail. After the bombing, he fled the country and hid in Northern Ireland for six years.

The lawyer's name was Marvin Kramer, a fourth-generation Mississippi Jew whose family had prospered as merchants in the Delta. He lived in an antebellum home in Greenville, a rivertown with a small but strong Jewish community, a pleasant place with a history of little racial discord. He practiced law because commerce bored him. Like most Jews of German descent, his family had assimilated nicely into the culture of the Deep South, and viewed themselves as nothing but typical Southerners who happened to have a different religion. Anti-Semitism rarely surfaced. For the most part, they blended with the rest of established society and went about their business.

antebellum before the Civil War

Marvin was different. His father sent him up North to Brandeis in the late Fifties. He spent four years there, then three years in Law School at Columbia and when he returned to Greenville in 1964 the civil rights movement had center stage in Mississippi. Marvin got in the thick of it. Less than a month after opening his little law office, he was arrested along with two of his Brandeis classmates for attempting to register black voters. His father was furious. His family was embarrassed, but Marvin couldn't have cared less. He received his first death threat at the age of twenty-five, and started carrying a gun. He bought a pistol for his wife, a Memphis girl, and instructed their black maid to keep one in her purse. The Kramers had twin two-year old sons.

Brandeis Jewish university in Massachusetts

Columbia university in New York

The first civil rights lawsuit filed in 1965 by the law offices of Marvin B. Kramer and Associates (there were no associates yet) alleged a multitude of discriminatory voting practices by local officials. It made headlines around the state, and Marvin got his picture in the papers. He also got his name on a Klan list of Jews to harass. Here was a radical Jew lawyer with a beard and a bleeding heart, educated by Jews up North and now marching with and representing Negroes in the Mississippi Delta. It would not be tolerated.

Klan Ku-Klux-Klan: anti-black, -Catholic, -Jewish organization, predominantly in the South

Later, there were rumors of Lawyer Kramer using his own money to post bail for Freedom Riders and civil rights workers. He filed lawsuits attacking whites-only facilities. He paid for the reconstruction of a black church bombed by the Klan. He was actually seen welcoming

Negroes into his home. He made speeches before Jewish groups up North and urged them to get involved in the struggle. He wrote sweeping letters to newspapers, few of which were printed. Lawyer Kramer was marching bravely toward his doom.

The presence of a nighttime guard patrolling benignly around the flower beds prevented an attack upon the Kramer home. Marvin had been paying the guard for two years. He was a former cop and he was heavily armed, and the Kramers let it be known to all of Greenville that they were protected by an expert marksman. Of course, the Klan knew about the guard, and the Klan knew to leave him alone. Thus, the decision was made to bomb Marvin Kramer's office, and not his home.

John Grisham: *The Chamber*, London and New York: BCA, 1994, pp. 1–2

Assignments

Your tasks are as follows:

1. Outline how Marvin Kramer's life and the general development of the United States in the sixties are related to one another.
2. Explain the particular reasons Grisham may have had to choose Marvin Kramer for his hero and to present him the way he did.
3. Show how the author manages to create an atmosphere of growing danger and rising antagonism.
4. Characterize point of view and tone of the opening passage.
5. After what you have read so far, *either*
   a) speculate on how the novel might continue, *or*
   b) write the next paragraph(s) of the exposition
   and briefly comment on a) or b).

Solutions

1. After a matter-of-fact report on the bombing of "the office of the radical Jew lawyer" (cf. frame of the first and the last paragraph) the reader hears about the life of Marvin Kramer, his Jewish background and Southern way of life as opposed to his own career: education in the North, his joining the Civil Rights Movement, law suits against local officials, support of the Civil Rights movement with his own money, social contacts with blacks and public speeches on their behalf – parallel to his rising commitment goes discrimination against him which leads to the threat to murder him mirrored in the increase of his own measures of self-defence.
2. M. K. is the "outsider par excellence", a Jew of German ancestry, educated at Northern universities, leftist liberal and anti-racist in the conservative, racist Deep South, a lawyer fighting for Civil Rights against the Klan terror, maintaining social contacts with blacks in a segregated society; though he belongs to a family of well-to-do assimilated Jews, he does not care about his family's pact with the establishment but rebels against it (ironical variant of the theme of segregation: the Jew as an outsider, the scapegoat, the hero fighting for his cause instead of the blind victim – cf. Isler).

3. Grisham links the style of a chronicler's neutral report on the events (as if he were writing on the history of the Civil Rights Movement) with a personal account of a man's fate; the frame on the bombing stresses the predictability and inevitability of this dramatic development; the dialectic structure of the text and the use of antitheses underline an antagonism that cannot be bridged: individual vs. majority, Jew vs. WASP, outsider vs. establishment, critical intellect abiding by the law vs. uncontrolled violent action; North vs. South, Civil Rights vs. white supremacy (Klan), alliance of Jew and blacks vs. white authorities, progress vs. traditionalism; repetition (he) and paratactic syntax to underline the factual, realistic (historical context) and the enumeration of the inevitable stages in this affair (dramatic tension), and the pointed statement at the end of the paragraph; the use of metaphors to express the tragical irony (with a beard and a bleeding heart, marching bravely toward his doom; living in an antebellum home – in a time of undeclared war on him), etc.

4. Mixture of chronicle (dates, places, persons), a biographical account (Who's Who) and a news story: neutral and objective, rather unbiased, only slight tendency to take Marvin's side and comment directly to guide the reader's sympathy (cf. under 3), use of irony); a change, e.g. to the point of view of a first-person narrator (insert "I" in ll. 8ff. or ll. 18ff. would automatically result in a much more personal tone and a story in which the historical development is no longer seen as the seedground of discrimination and persecution but only serves as a historical facade before which the drama of an individual unfolds), choosing the neutral point of view and a matter-of-fact tone shows the inseparable connection between a social climate, public opinion and the fate of the individual.

5. A piece of creative writing combined with a reflection on one's own writing (ideas, themes, motifs, use of language, e.g. dialogue, etc.).

Klausur 2

Part 1: Responding to an advertisement

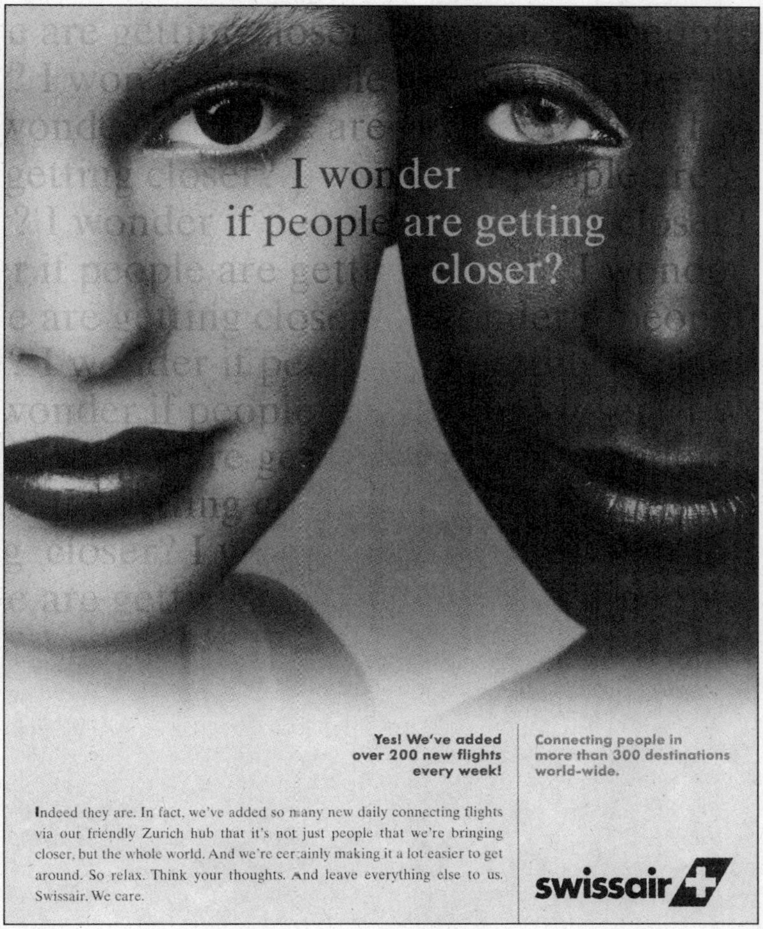

Assignments

Your task is as follows:

This advertisement announces more daily connecting flights worldwide. First, describe how you personally respond to the eyecatcher. Then comment on the strategy behind the advertisement.

Part 2: Responding to a text

Healthy, Wealthy and Unhappy

Why is it that economic success does not necessarily bring personal contentment?

fertilizer used to improve the quality of the soil

to cohabit to live together

empirical based on fact and experience

GDP (gross domestic product) value of all goods and services produced in the economy

carpenter of Galilee Jesus Christ
blinkers *Scheuklappen*
cerebral relating to the brain
visceral dealing with emotions
scrutiny analysis
pursuit of happiness human right granted in the American Declaration of Independence
Pace here: forget about
Epicurus who thought intellectual pleasures the highest

Some years ago, the story goes, a large corporation gave African peasants fertilizer so that their crop would double. And indeed it did. The businessmen thought they had sown the seeds of efficient agriculture. Alas, when the next season came the peasants didn't plant anything. "Why don't you plant?" the businessmen asked. The peasants thought this somewhat silly. "Our last harvest was double," they replied. "We have enough to feed our families till next year." Whether a rural legend or not, the story illustrates the different answers people give to the question, How much does man need? One says, "Enough to subsist." Another may say, "As much as possible." The latter certainly creates more wealth. But does he also create more happiness?

Any seasoned traveler can attest to the fact that wealth and happiness do not usually cohabit. Visit Europe and be mystified by the unsmiling faces and furrowed brows in the most affluent countries. Visit Africa and marvel at the laughter and general merriment, even in the most impoverished ones.

For those who prefer empirical to impressionistic evidence, there are opinion polls. I recall that back in the '80s, a survey asked Western Europeans the mother of all questions: Are you happy? The Germans, the richest, were the most miserable. The Irish and Portuguese, the poorest, turned out to be the most contented. In 1998, a global survey by the Angus Reid Group constructed a Hope Index, asking people how optimistic they felt about the future. Pessimism reigned supreme in Europe, particularly in the countries along the Rhine. In Germany (per capita GDP $ 28,000) only 18% of the respondents were upbeat about the future, and in France ($ 26,000) it was 17%. By comparison, South Africa ($ 3,500) and Brazil ($ 4,400) scored 42% and 64% on the Hope Index. It is not a new insight that the relationship between material and emotional welfare seems to be an inverse one. When the carpenter of Galilee declared that man does not live by bread alone, he reminded all those who see man as *Homo oeconomicus* of their materialist blinkers.

What is the explanation for this strange phenomenon? Maybe it has to do with the cerebral and the visceral. Mankind has known for a long time that too much self-scrutiny is not conducive to happiness. "Ask yourself whether you are happy, and you cease to be so," John Stuart Mill wrote more than 100 years ago. To intellectuals, the pursuit of happiness is something unbecoming of cultured people. It is appropriate, the élite might argue, only to the shallow and the unsophisticated. How many novels or movies about happy people win critical aclaim? Anguish and discontent are taken as the mark of a deep thinker, a well-rehearsed frown as his badge. *Pace* Epicurus, a happy intellectual is an oxymoron.

Gerd Behrens, Time, July 19, 1999, p. 76

Your tasks are as follows:

Assignments

1. State to what extent the parable in the opening paragraph sums up the gist of the article.
2. According to the author's explanation of the phenomenon "a happy intellectual is an oxymoron." Show how he makes his point.
3. Frequent references are made to the Germans' state of mind. Voice your approval or disapproval in a letter to the editor taking into account some different American and European behaviours.

Solutions

Part 1

Attracted by the beautiful expressive faces that, only on the face of things, stand for a divided world. The provocative rhetorical question right in the centre is answered by the message of the picture: Intimate contact, cheek to cheek, indicates closeness and togetherness: The gap between races, ethnic groups or continents has been bridged. Even physical features such as brown or blue eyes are interchangeable to underline the unity between the two as representatives of worlds formerly apart. The strategy makes use of the emotional connotations and associations to make the business of an airline look like a humanitarian programme. Selling through creating sympathy, international-mindedness, solidarity.

Part 2

1. Obvious contrast between economic reasoning and human feeling, between future-directedness and a *carpe-diem-* mentality, between intellect and soul, head and heart, the "cerebral and the visceral." And in a wider context, the conflict betwen scientific, industrial and technological progress of the Western world and the claim to follow their own Third-World standards.
2. Mainly through dialectic argument, the use of antitheses, e.g. Europe/America – Africa, ordinary people enjoying life – pessimistic materialist élite unable to pursue happiness; the visceral: warm heart and soul – the cerebral: cold intellect; simplicity of thought and language of the parable and reference to the "carpenter of Galilee" – complexity and sophistication of Western philosophy (Epicurus, J. Stuart Mill) and "disgust"; it all amounts to the incompatibility of different worlds (good – bad), a nostalgic, idealistic, romantic view of the past (civilizational and cultural lag of Africa: Africa's present age – our past). It is all underlined by a language that antagonizes simplicity and sophistication.
3. The student can make reference to some American culture standards that underly Behrens' argument, the general distrust of essential European behaviours: e.g. theory before practice, intellectual distrust of emotions, duty and obligations before fun and happiness, concern about the future before enjoying the simple plea-

sures of life, etc. A letter to the editor might partly agree with the author's criticism of an intellectual paralysis, but can stress the complexity of some of the problems of a modern world (overpopulation, scarcity of resources, global threat of ideologies, wars, malnutrition, disease, etc. – cf. There is a simple solution to every complex problem: The wrong one.) and can point out some of specific German reasons for this attitude (see Lord's term of "Nazi experience", see also a system of education that used to concentrate on the intellect only), but should also state that the young generation shares a different, more global outlook with young people all over the world and has many values in common with them.